The Economics of Planning

R. KERRY TURNER
Research Fellow, Public Sector Economics Research Centre, University of Leicester

and

CLIVE COLLIS
Principal Lecturer in Economics, Lanchester Polytechnic

M

First published 1977 by
THE MACMILLAN PRESS LTD
London and Basingstoke
Associated companies in New York Dublin Melbourne Johannesburg and Madras

ISBN 0 333 19657 0

Typeset in Great Britain by
PREFACE GRAPHICS LTD
Salisbury, Wilts.
Printed in Great Britain by
UNWIN BROTHERS LIMITED
The Gresham Press, Old Woking, Surrey

Editors' Preface to Macmillan Studies in Economics

The rapid growth of academic literature in the field of economics has posed serious problems for both students and teachers of the subject. The latter find it difficult to keep pace with more than a few areas of the subject so that an inevitable trend towards specialism emerges. The student quickly loses perspective as the maze of theories and models grows, particularly at a time when so much reappraisal of the established paradigms is taking place.

The aim of the 'Macmillan Studies in Economics' is to offer students, and perhaps some teachers as well, short, reasonably critical overviews of developments in selected areas of economics, particularly those in which current controversies are to be found. As far as possible the titles have been selected to form an integrated whole, although inevitably entire areas have been neglected as being unsuited to the style, format and length of the titles in the series.

In some cases the volumes are rather more like essays than surveys. In most cases, however, the aim is to survey the salient literature in a critical fashion. The level of understanding required to read the volumes varies with the complexity of the subject, but they have been generally written to suit the second- and third-year undergraduate seeking to place his reading of the detailed literature in an over-all context. They are *not* textbooks. Instead they seek to give the kind of perspective that might well be lost by reading longer textbooks on their own, or by reading articles in journals. In particular, they should be most suited to pre-examination revision periods. They are not intended to substitute for the essential reading and assimilation of the original works that they seek to survey and assess.

MACMILLAN STUDIES IN ECONOMICS

General Editors: D. C. ROWAN and G. R. FISHER

Executive Editor: D. W. PEARCE

Published

R. W. Anderson: THE ECONOMICS OF CRIME
John Burton: WAGE INFLATION
Ben Fine: MARX'S 'CAPITAL'
Douglas Fisher: MONETARY POLICY
Miles Fleming: MONETARY THEORY
C. J. Hawkins and D. W. Pearce: CAPITAL INVESTMENT APPRAISAL
C. J. Hawins: THEORY OF THE FIRM
David F. Heathfield: PRODUCTION FUNCTIONS
Dudley Jackson: POVERTY
P. N. Junankar: INVESTMENT: THEORIES AND EVIDENCE
J. E. King: LABOUR ECONOMICS
John King and Philip Regan: RELATIVE INCOME SHARES
J. A. Kregel: THE THEORY OF ECONOMIC GROWTH
J. A. Kregel: THEORY OF CAPITAL
Richard Lecomber: ECONOMIC GROWTH VERSUS THE ENVIRONMENT
George McKenzie: THE MONETARY THEORY OF INTERNATIONAL TRADE
David J. Mayston: THE IDEA OF SOCIAL CHOICE
C. A. Nash: PUBLIC VERSUS PRIVATE TRANSPORT
S. K. Nath: A PERSPECTIVE OF WELFARE ECONOMICS
Anthony Peaker: ECONOMIC GROWTH IN MODERN BRITAIN
D. W. Pearce: COST-BENEFIT ANALYSIS
Maurice Peston: PUBLIC GOODS AND THE PUBLIC SECTOR
Nicholas Rau: TRADE CYCLES: THEORY AND PRACTICE
David Robertson: INTERNATIONAL TRADE POLICY
Charles K. Rowley: ANTITRUST AND ECONOMIC EFFICIENCY
C. H. Sharp: TRANSPORT ECONOMICS
G. K. Shaw: FISCAL POLICY
R. Shone: THE PURE THEORY OF INTERNATIONAL TRADE
M. J. Stabler: AGRICULTURAL ECONOMICS AND RURAL LAND-USE
Frank J. B. Stilwell: REGIONAL ECONOMIC POLICY
A. P. Thirlwall: FINANCING ECONOMIC DEVELOPMENT
R. Kerry Turner and Clive Collis: THE ECONOMICS OF PLANNING
John Vaizey: THE ECONOMICS OF EDUCATION
J. van Doorn: DISEQUILIBRIUM ECONOMICS
Peter A. Victor: ECONOMICS OF POLLUTION
Graham Walshe: INTERNATIONAL MONETARY REFORM
Michael G. Webb: PRICING POLICIES FOR PUBLIC ENTERPRISES
E. Roy Weintraub: CONFLICT AND CO-OPERATION IN ECONOMICS
E. Roy Weintraub: GENERAL EQUILIBRIUM THEORY

Forthcoming

Susan Charles: HOUSING ECONOMICS
A. Ziderman: MANPOWER TRAINING: THEORY AND POLICY

Contents

Acknowledgements

We wish to thank David Pearce and Silvan Jones for reading and commenting on earlier versions, and Pat Greatorex of the Public Sector Economics Research Centre, Leicester, for her admirable typing.

R. K. T.
C. M. C.

Introduction

This book is a survey of the main forms of economic planning in both Western market economies and the socialist economies of the Soviet Union and Eastern Europe. The planning models discussed include both empirical and theoretical variants of the basic indicative and imperative planning systems.

After the abortive planning exercise of the 1960s the present (1977) Labour government is currently investigating the idea of 'planning agreements' with industry. In the light of this it is interesting to look at the reasons for the failure of the U.K. *National Plan* and by contrast the comparative success of the French planning system. Economic planning is of course synonymous with the Soviet Union and post-war Eastern Europe. However, since the 1960s 'new' theories and forms of planning have begun to emerge. The central feature of many of the 'new' socialist planning theories has been the emphasis placed on the simultaneous operation of a constrained market mechanism and central planning.

Chapter 1 summarises the main arguments that have taken place in the literature on the relationship between planning and the market mechanism. It concludes with a suggested taxonomy of planning systems which provides an over-all framework for the analysis of individual systems.

Chapters 2 and 3 analyse both the theoretical basis and the actual operation of the socialist planning systems. Chapters 4 and 5 are devoted to a similar exercise for the indicative planning systems that currently still operates in France and used to function in the United Kingdom in the 1960s.

1 Planning and the Market Mechanism

Any economic analysis of national economic planning necessarily involves a discussion of the relative merits of, and relationship between, the market and planning. This chapter outlines the main arguments that have taken place in the literature on the issues. It concludes with a suggested framework within which different planning systems can be discussed.

Belief in the virtues of a free market economy has a long history. The classical economists argued that, with certain minimal functions for government (notably law and order), the freely operating market system would secure social well-being through the individual pursuit of self-interest [1]. Modern welfare economics has demonstrated that, given certain assumptions [2], a perfectly competitive market economy in equilibrium is sufficient to meet the necessary conditions for the achievement of Pareto optimality. In so far as the assumptions are unrealistic—for example, the world is not one of universal perfect competition—there are natural monopolies, there are externalities and public goods, there is imperfect information about the present and uncertainty about the future—a role is ascribed to government to correct for market failures. Moreover, for each different income distribution there exists a particular Paretian optimum, and a judgement that the existing distribution is inequitable would provide a further case for government intervention. Furthermore, fulfilment of the objectives of full employment, price stability and faster economic growth ensures that in modern market economies considerable government intervention takes place at the microeconomic and macroeconomic levels.

Intervention in the form of indicative planning takes place currently in France although there was a U.K.

experiment in the 1960s. The advocates of indicative planning argue that the existence of uncertainty about the future provides a rationale for planning to complement the market mechanism. Additionally, if a faster rate of economic growth is desired, indicative planning is advocated as an extra weapon complementary to conventional economic policy [3,4,5]. However, the role of planning in a market economy is an area of some dispute. Some regard indicative planning as a peril [6]; some regard the theory of indicative planning as a logically invalid demonstration of the need for planning in a market economy [7,8]; others argue that in principle and in practice indicative planning can complement the market and conventional economic policy [9].

Although perfect competition is a sufficient condition for the achievement of a Paretian optimum, it is not a necessary condition. The conditions necessary for Pareto optimality are also met by an appropriately designed planned socialist economy containing state-owned enterprises. Lange's 'competitive socialism' model,* characterised by marginal-cost pricing, represents an attempt to set up a theoretical but feasible socialist solution; it forms part of an historic debate, the 'socialist controversy'. Disputants argued whether a socialist solution was theoretically possible, whether it was practicable in terms of informational requirements once the market was replaced, as well as whether a socialist system can be more efficient than a market economy. Writers such as Dobb and Dickenson [10] argued that if planning is of a sufficiently high standard, if it is consistent and efficient, there would be no need for any other control; in particular it would be unnecessary to expose the economy to market-induced fluctuations and frictions.

In the real world the Soviet approach to planning evolved from the basic principle of social ownership of the means of production, the accepted premise being that economic instruments of indirect control (money, credit and taxation)

* An excellent summary of the 'socialist controversy' debate appears in [10].

are not dependable and will not guarantee an economy progressing towards the attainment of predetermined centrally laid-down goals—hence the Soviet reliance on direct guidance through imperative planning, information flowing vertically through the system with central control taking the form of directives (commands) expressed in physical terms. However, the Hungarian economist Kornai [11] argues that both the extreme 'market' view and the extreme 'central plan' view can only be validated by using the same set of restrictive assumptions, He concludes that neither the market nor planning can in isolation control a modern complex economic system: what is required is a combination of the two control sub-systems [12]. A number of practical attempts to achieve just such a control combination are now under way in some of the socialist economies of Eastern Europe.

A TAXONOMY OF PLANNING SYSTEMS

In this section we will attempt to distinguish between a number of planning systems which vary according to the type of organisational structure established, the type of messages (information) which that system is supposed to process, and the scale of preferences that dominates the system. It is necessary right at the start to bear in mind that every classification framework yet attempted is an oversimplification of empirical planning systems. The exercise itself nevertheless performs a useful descriptive role.

Progress in the attempt to construct a conceptual frame for all the variants of planning systems has been limited. Two polar types can possibly be identified, the 'Soviet type', developed under Stalin since 1928, and the 'French type', the indicative planning system. In terms of practical approximation the former has come as close as feasible to a fully state-administered, centrally directed socialist economy; the latter to a state-guided, market-directed and largely private-enterprise economy. The classification system we are going to use is based on the degree of centralisation and concentration implicit in the planning systems [13,14] and on the distinction between postulational and empirical planning systems. Postulational systems illustrate efficiently functioning economies and are used to work out optimal solutions and contain assumptions which may or may not fit in with the reality of the actual planning process operating in an economy. On the other hand, empirical systems are the real-world systems of planning. The concepts of centralisation and decentralisation unfortunately pose far more difficult definitional problems, numerous definitions having been proposed over the years.

There is the 'informational' approach associated with the work of Hurwicz [15] and others, the aim of this group of economists being the formulation of abstract models of planning systems. Hurwicz makes the assumption that at the beginning of a resource-allocation process all economic information is dispersed throughout the economy, each individual economic unit having perfect information concerning itself (its production function, preferences and resources) and no information concerning the other units. During the allocative process, however, communication will take place between the units before decisions are taken and acted upon. It is the communication stage that Hurwicz concentrates on when defining 'informational' decentralisation as communication requiring transfers of about as much information as would ordinarily be transmitted under the free-market organisation, that is transfers of commodity-dimensional messages, in other words price and output data only. Hurwicz sees the decentralised and centralised allocative processes as polar extreme cases. At the opposite end of the continuum from complete 'informational' decentralisation lies the polar centralised system in which all dispersed information, not just price and output data, is transmitted and held by a single central authority or central planning board (C.P.B.). The C.P.B. then calculates the production flows and takes over the decision-making role.

Following on from Hayek's contention that such a transfer of dispersed information to the C.P.B. is not feasible, the complexity of the information ruling out on practical grounds any national calculations, a number of postulational decentralised planning procedures have been developed which are not competitive price systems. The earliest of these models was Lange's 'competitive solution' (see Chapter 2); subsequent advances in economic theory, particularly mathematical economic theory, have led Hurwicz and others to develop more complex systems. All the systems involve an exchange of information between a C.P.B. and the various economic units in the form of an iterative process, with some calculations being made by the individual units. These models were originally derived from technical advances made in the field of large-scale, linear-programming problems, in particular the development of decomposition algorithms by Dantzig and Wolfe (see Chapter 2). The algorithms can be interpreted as models of multi-level planning processes [16].

Actual planning systems, however, do not fit neatly and precisely into the 'informational' systems framework. The different empirical variants of socialist planning presumably are closer to the centralised end of the continuum, the Yugoslav system being furthest away while Western indicative planning would be located closer to the decentralisedend. Albin [17] argues that at first glance indicative plannning fits naturally into the category of decentralised information systems; and, as Lecomber [18] points out, pure indicative planning theory indicates that its purpose is to organise an interchange of information ultimately arriving at a co-ordinated system of individual decision-makers' plans, not by coercion but by the recognition of mutual self-interests. However, both writers conclude that a large amount of additional information (over and above commodity-dimensional messages) needs to be communicated between decision-makers and planners. Thus the indicative planning system would appear to be centralised in terms of the 'informational' approach to the concept. Furthermore, any differences between Yugoslav planning practices and the French indicative system would appear to be small.

A second approach to the problem of defining centralisation can be labelled the 'decision-making-authority' approach and is associated with the work of Montias, among others [19,20,21]. This group attempts to derive conclusions from the study of actual planning systems. Empirically, they argue, socialist planning systems operate with a variety of organisations but usually within a hierarchical framework. The 'authority' approach concentrates on the relation between economic units in which one is 'in authority' over another 'with respect to a particular activity', that is issues commands backed by sanctions specifying the outcome of another unit's decision or set of decisions. Thus what is actually being analysed is the administrative structure of the planning system. The concept of a hierarchical decision-making structure incorporating many levels serves as a useful approximation to reality. Thus according to the 'authority' approach the process of decentralisation is one in which decisions are delegated from a superior level in the hierarchy to a subordinate level lower down. Using this approach French indicative planning would appear to be highly decentralised, with the Yugoslav variant of socialist planning also containing a fair measure of decentralisation.

Kornai, however, conceives of two types of superior/subordinate relations [11]. There is the 'directive-based' relationship but also the 'indispensable-information-based' relationship. In the latter case a planning office would have a monopoly on issuing central-plan information vital to the functioning of the system, and this would be the cause even in an indicative planning environment. All empirical economic systems, Kornai argues, are multi-level, and can be differentiated in terms of the importance of the vertical or horizontal relationships and flows of information that they contain. Vertical relationships became more important in market systems as the role of government became more interventionist, eventually ending up with indicative planning, these relationships being predominantly of a non-directive nature. In the socialist systems directive relationships are important but their significance varies from country to country. In terms of information flows both indicative and socialist central-planning systems contain horizontal and vertical flows but the latter predominate in socialist systems and the former in indicative systems.

A third possible approach to defining centralisation takes the system of preferences governing the national economy as the decisive criterion. Thus we can conceive of an economic system that is governed by the centre's set of preferences or planners' sovereignty. Decentralisation can then be defined as a movement toward an economic system governed by consumer preferences, or an extension of consumers' choice under planners' sovereignty. Keizer [14] is concerned to distinguish carefully between centralisation and a concept he terms 'concentration'; concentration refers to the extent to which the centre takes charge of all detailed microeconomic decisions as well as general macroeconomic policy decisions. 'Deconcentration' refers to the process of delegation of the centre's decision-making powers to lower levels in the administrative hierarchy, eventually ending up with individual producers and consumers. It would seem that what Keizer has in mind is similar if not identical to the 'authority' approach to the concept of decentralisation.

Two further concepts can be defined. First, there is 'administrative deconcentration', which is merely the delegation of decision-making to subordinate administrative units, that is the creation of an administrative network in order to aid the efficient operation of the over-all economic system, in Zielinski's terminology [22], the creation of a 'non-parametric management mechanism', the centre using mainly directives and not price signals to transmit information to plan executants. Second, there is 'parametric deconcentration', which involves the delegation of decision-making authority to individual plan executants who respond to centrally determined parameters. This 'parametric management mechanism' guides plan executants by changing economic parameters like wages, prices and taxes. It is also possible to distinguish between

TABLE 1

The model	*Degree of centralisation*	*Degree of concentration*	*Postulational/empirical*
Traditional Stalinist model (Soviet Union 1928–mid-1950s)	Rigid centralisation A directive/bureaucratic model	Partial administrative deconcentration 'Ministerial' administrative system	Empirical Adopted by East European satellite economies in the late 1940s and to a large extent still operated by Albania
Reformed Soviet model (1960s, 1970s)	Less rigid centralisation A technocratic model	Administrative and state parametric deconcentration Sovnarkohzy system 1957–65 'Flexible' ministerial system (post-1965) 'Industrial association' system developed in Eastern Europe	Empirical Adopted by East Germany, Rumania and Poland
Guided market model	Partial decentralisation A managerial model	Parametric deconcentration, the market being given some part to play in resource allocation	Empirical Adopted in Hungary (1968) and operated for a short time in Czechoslovakia and Bulgaria
Supplemented market model	Decentralised model Workers collective model	Market parametric deconcentration	Empirical The Yugoslav system

Indicative planning model	Decentralised model	Highly deconcentrated market parametric	Empirical Operates in France and influenced planning in other E.E.C. economies particularly the United Kingdom in the 1960s
Pure indicative planning	Decentralised model	Highly deconcentrated	Postulational
Soviet cybernetic administrative model of Gostekhnika	Centralised model	Ideally with perfect concentration	Postulational
Soviet programming models of the T.S.E.M.I.	Partially decentralised models	Parametric deconcentration, the market being given some role to play	Postulational
Lange type 'competitive socialist' models	Decentralised and partially decentralised models	Parametric deconcentration Lange model [37] – market parametric – Sik's model [40] (Czechoslovakia) Brus's model [38] (Poland)	Postulational

'state-parametric' and 'market-parametric' management mechanisms. A movement towards the use of a 'market-parametric' mechanism involves plan executants responding to consumer and not centrally determined parameters.

Having attempted a list of definitions it is important to note again that none of the above are totally unambiguous or totally realistic when reference is made to actual planning systems [23]. Nevertheless, the concepts are useful, despite their lack of precision, in indicating the overall direction of change which may be taking place in a planning system. Table 1 summarises the main planning systems in terms of the degree of centralisation, taking the preference approach to the concept, and the degree of concentration implicit in the system.

2 Socialist Planning Theory

Socialist planning theory has evolved as one part of a general and as yet incomplete 'theory of the socialist economy'. All socialist countries subscribe to some interpretation of a Marxist-Leninist economic philosophy; the Soviet Union was the first country to adopt such a philosophy as its only recognised economic doctrine, the transition from mainstream Western economic thought being complete by 1930. There are many definitions of a 'socialist' economy in the literature; Lavigne [24] is critical of a number of these and puts forward her own version based on one central criterion, social ownership of the basic means of production. Given this basic condition the achievement of the two central aims—state domination of the systems in terms of the ruling preferences and imperative central planning—has been possible.

MARXIAN ECONOMIC HERITAGE

It has often been pointed out that in dealing with planned socialist economies techniques developed to study Western market economies are not very relevant; and furthermore, that just as the principles of catalytic theory were derived from the economic goals of market economies, the parallel principles for socialist economies ought to be derived from the ideological, political and economic goals of those systems. Taking the Soviet economic system as our model we find a complex set of goals in existence. By 1930 the Soviet Union had fully adopted the Marxian economic doctrine; however, in theoretical terms this heritage proved to be extremely limited. Marx had not mapped out a detailed blueprint for a future socialist society. His main concern had been the formulation of a critique of capitalism. Both Lenin and Stalin had to reinterpret and adapt Marx's writings.

SOVIET REINTERPRETATION OF MARX

During the Stalinist era the economy was put through a period of planned and rapid economic growth. Planning in physical terms was the practical approach adopted and economists and economic theory were pushed well into the back ground. After going as far as abolishing the 'law' of value—the forces of supply and demand—Stalin later reinstated it within the political economy of socialism, although limiting its sphere of operation to the private consumption sector and relegating the price system to an auxiliary role. By the 'value' of a commodity Marxists mean the amount of 'socially necessary' labour time embodied in the product. However, the Soviet planners did not necessarily set the prices of goods equal to the 'value' of the goods. The price system that developed played a purely accounting role in the economy and was not allowed to determine the allocation of resources. In the Marxian scheme the value of a commodity consists of three parts: constant capital (c), the value of depreciation plus the raw materials used up in the production process; variable capital (v), the value of labour power used up (wages); and surplus value (s) created by labour in the system and expropriated by the capitalist entrepreneur, the rate of exploitation being s/v. Thus the rudimentary Marxian price formula reads: $p = c + v + s$. Using this as a base, Soviet producer prices were normally set at the cost of the average enterprise in the industry concerned plus a normal profit mark-up. Consumer-good prices were set at a level to establish an equilibrium between supply and demand, that is, at market-clearing prices. During the Stalinist period, however, the price system did degenerate into an arbitrary set of price relationships with little economic meaning [25].

The arbitrary price system caused severe problems in the capital-goods sector. At the macroeconomic level in the early years of the planning era, no formal efficiency criteria were used to rank investment projects. This situation was justified on the Marxist grounds that capital as a factor of production contributes nothing to production. At the microeconomic level, enterprises wasted capital equipment which in reality was productive and was also scarce in relation to requirements. Thus at the operational level there remained the problem of using scarce capital resources in the most productive way, and rules for capital allocation gradually developed. After a period of relying on engineering data, economic criteria re-established themselves. By the 1960s Soviet methodology was using two basic investment criteria—the criterion of general or absolute efficiency, which is the marginal output-capital ratio, and the so-called 'pay-off-period' criterion. The latter evaluates variants of a given investment project in terms of the length of time it takes a more capital-intensive variant, through lower operating costs, to recoup its higher initial capital costs [26, 27, 28].

Towards the end of the 1950s a number of theoretical discussions emerged on the question of the construction of a more rational price system. Three schools of thought can be isolated: the labour-cost approach, whereby prices should be set in proportion to labour costs; the 'cost-plus' school, according to which prices should be set in proportion to the cost of production plus a profit mark-up; and the planometric optimising approach, which maintains that the prices of the means of production should be proportional to their marginal productivity, an approach that sees price determination as part of the over-all problem of a national optimal planning system. Actual price reforms were initiated in the period 1960—7 but the new system has not substantially modified existing practice and the Soviet Union still does not possess a rational system of scarcity prices.

The economists who survived the purges of the 1930s were given the task of interpreting the political economy of socialism. Whenever convenient to the leadership various universal 'laws' of socialism, broadly derived from Marxian ideas, were invoked in order to justify *ex post* the evolving empirical economic system. At the operational level the

Soviet leadership, their planners and engineers, encountered and attempted to solve a wide range of problems. Thus a body of empirically constructed principles emerged which, once 'justified' in political terms, served as a theoretical basis for planning decisions. Campbell [27] and Wilczynski [29] note, however, that these empirically evolved principles have never coalesced into a general theory of allocation and value. The Soviet leadership replaced the 'anarchy of the market' with the 'conscious and organized use of economic laws under socialism' and the law of planned proportional development of the national economy. The latter is necessary in order that the ultimate communist state of abundance be achieved sometime in the future and on the more practical grounds of overtaking, as quickly as possible, the advanced Western economies. The law of planned proportional development lays down that in order to maximise the over-all rate of growth of the economy, the capital-goods sector should get priority in terms of investment resources at the expense of present consumption levels. In Soviet terminology, department one or *A*, the producer-goods sector, must grow at a faster rate than department two or *B*, the consumer-goods sector. This Stalinist growth model has its origins in the Marxian 'reproduction' scheme [30], although Marx himself did not lay down what the relative sectoral rates of growth should be. It was left to Lenin originally and then Stalin to lay down that department one (*a*) should be given priority in order to boost the production of producer goods necessary to produce further producer goods.

Theoretically Feld'man had formulated just such a rudimentary two-sector model in the Soviet economic debates of the 1920s.* For Feld'man the rate of growth of an economy is dependent on the proportionate size of the capital-goods sector net of depreciation multiplied by the 'effectiveness of capital', which is the capital-output ratio. The only factor which limits growth in the model is capital; labour supplies are assumed to be unlimited. For a survey of the debates in the 1920s see Erlich [32] and Nove [33].

* The Feld'man model is discussed in [31].

In his critique of capitalism Marx had noted that, due to technological change, the so-called 'organic composition of capital' was rising over time. This is the ratio of constant capital to variable capital (c/v), equivalent in Western terms to the capital—labour ratio (K/L). Now Lenin linked together the 'law' of a rising organic composition of capital with his own reformulation of Marx's 'reproduction schema to produce the 'law' of proportionate development. This implied view of the effect of technological progress, a labour-saving, capital-absorptive view, was held to be universal. Lawson [30] points out that the rule does not rigidly lay down which industries should be preferred; in fact, Soviet planning doctrine interprets the rule as calling for faster growth in the energy and heavy industries. The planner can regulate the entire economic system through two sectoral pairs of parameters, in Zauberman's terminology [26], the 'sectoral accelerators': (*a*) the ratio at which surplus product (s) is diverted into capital formation in sectors one and two; and (*b*) the sectoral organic composition of capital ratios.

Thus in terms of long-term planning, an 'extensive-type' growth strategy was adopted, that is emphasis was placed on the creation of massive amounts of additional productive capacity [34]. Unlike indicative planning, in which plan construction begins with the estimation of final demands for the terminal year and then involves calculating sectoral outputs and inputs to meet the demands, traditional Soviet planning practice is supply-side and not demand-side planning. The starting-point for the Soviet planner was a set of given gross output targets for official 'priority' goods. The so-called 'leading links' method of planning was adopted; production plans for other goods were structured around the target outputs for the priority industries and their inputs.

THE 'SOCIALIST CONTROVERSY' DEBATE

In our search for the underlying economic principles of the 'theory of the socialist economy', we have taken as our model the Soviet system as it evolved in the 1920s and 1930s. In fact, the earliest debates among Western economists on the 'socialist controversy' took place before the creation of the Soviet state. In 1908 Barone demonstrated that a centrally administered socialist economic system could allocate resources efficiently if the centre had perfect knowledge of the aggregate resource base, the preference systems existing and finally the production function for each level of output; and further, if the centre had the technical capability necessary to solve the millions of equations needed to arrive at a general-equilibrium situation. Barone's optimality criterion is the Pareto optimum of social welfare.

In the early 1920s von Mises argued that no system of rational prices could be arrived at without a market mechanism. Later, Hayek stressed the practical impossibility of the centre computing all the equations and collecting the information necessary if the market was to be replaced.* Before 1940 two further schools of thought had emerged to challenge the von Mises—Hayek position. Lange offered his so-called 'competitive solution', the creation of a 'market socialist' system based on two main principles: social ownership of the basic means of production and minimum central control over the socialist productive enterprises and the individual households. A C.P.B. would be set up to take over the price-setting role of the market, equilibrium prices eventually being achieved after a process of trial and error—socialist *tatonnement*. The system could function in a decentralised fashion in the sense that consumer preferences would be satisfied, consumers attemting to maximise their utility and treating the C.P.B. prices as parameters. There would, however, be some check on consumer preferences due to the intervention by the C.P.B. in the system in order to influence the rate of investment. Parametric deconcentration would be present, with socialist enterprise managers and industrial authorities deciding on output levels and being guided only

* A brief summary of the views of Barone, von Mises and Hayek can be found in [10, ch. 9].

by two centrally laid-down rules leading to profit maximisation: (*a*) the marginal-cost pricing rule; and (*b*) the minimum average cost of production rule.

Lange claimed that his system solved the information/computation complexity problem, the C.P.B. not being required to know detailed microeconomic data and further having to carry a much reduced administrative burden due to the deconcentrated nature of the system. Subsequently a number of criticisms of the Lange model have been made in the literature [35]. A second school of thought, principally associated with the names of Dickenson and Dobb, offered the 'centralist solution' [10]. Dobb takes the position that a centrally planned socialist economy will prove superior to its competitive rival in three major areas: stimulating economic growth; maintaining balanced economic development; and finally, with the aid of modern computer technology, constructing an adequate, if not optimum, price system.

Each of the systems proposed in the debate in its pure and perfect form is theoretically capable of reaching static efficiency, a Pareto-optimum condition. Keizer [14] points out, however, that the Paretian welfare-optimum criterion is not the objective function for the Soviet economy, that in fact the objective function is not a purely economic entity but contains political and social factors which makes it inherently difficult to quantify. Drewnowski [36] criticised Lange's model on the grounds that it was not based on an analysis of actual socialist economies. He attempted to examine the question of the preference systems that actually exist in socialist economies. He establishes a dual preference system approach to the theory of socialist economies, a multiple system of individuals' preferences existing alongside a single state preference function. He argues that the vital problem of the theory of the socialist economy is the interaction between the state and individuals' preferences, offering a range of possible economic systems containing different plan-market combinations.

Nevertheless, Lange's model has served as the doctrinal basis of a number of more recent theoretical attempts to synthesise planning and the market mechanism. (For a survey of Lange's contributions to the economic theory of socialism, see Feiwel [37],) The Polish economist, Brus [38], has constructed a model of a planned economy containing a stage-regulated market mechanism, prices being fixed by the centre directly or through the use of indirect economic instruments. The model thus contains a measure of state-parametric deconcentration. Brus differs from Lange in the critical area of investment allocation; he argues that basic investment flows should be centrally controlled, emphasising the need for a co-ordinated investment programme in line with one of Dobb's criticisms of the Lange model [39].

The Czech economist, Sik [40], has formulated a model which contains a mixture of state- and market-parametric deconcentration. The central plan would operate basically at the macroeconomic level, and only the general price level and the prices of certain basic products would be regulated centrally. Any tendency towards monopoly in supply or speculative price increases would be countered by the use of indirect economic instruments. Towards the end of the 1950s Ward [41] put forward the so-called 'co-operative socialism' model in which the market is given a significant role to play in resource allocation. Co-operative enterprises run by worker groups operate autonomous production and employment policies and seek to maximise net earnings per worker. All productive assets are, however, owned by the state, which levies a tax on their use. Central control is limited to the public sector of the economy, using certain indirect economic instruments. Ward himself lists a number of criticisms of the model and doubts its practicability. Vanek [42], nevertheless, argues that in its perfectly competitive form the model is just as efficient as the perfectly competitive market system; furthermore, it is superior in terms of the distribution of factor rewards which is controlled by the co-operative workers collectively. However, the operation of the model in conditions of imperfect competition is the subject of some dispute [43]. The construction of both theoretical and less comprehensive empirical synthesised plan and market systems had led to an awareness among East European economists of the need for the formulation of an independent theory of socialist economic policy separate from 'socialist political economy' or 'planning theory'. (See Csikos-Nagy [44] for an attempt to outline the basic theory.)

By the 1950s the Soviet economy had matured considerably, setting the centre much more complex planning and control problems. There was a need for a shift in emphasis away from the 'extensive' growth strategy to a more intensive approach, that is, maximising growth via increases in over-all productivity. The latter approach required a much more sophisticated set of planning techniques. Furthermore, a number of the European satellite economies created after the Second World War already possessed fairly complex industrial sectors and foreign trade arrangements. The relatively autarkic Stalinist planning model did not prove appropriate given these conditions, the basis for this hypothesis being the declining growth rates of the socialist economies after 1959.

The question of Stalin's particular interpretation of the 'law' of proportionate development was raised after his death by the Polish economist, Kalecki [45]. He constructed what he termed an outline of the theory of economic growth in a centrally planned socialist economy. His work stressed the inevitable conflict between current consumption and the selection of high over-all rates of growth. Kalecki argued that the implied tenet seized on first by Lenin was not in fact a valid generalisation to make. He refuted the Marxist-Leninist conception of technological advance and pointed out that technical progress can be capital-saving, absorptive or neutral. The 'law' applies only if the capital-output ratio is rising and/or if economic growth is not just steady but accelerating. Kalecki's growth model highlights a number of constraints operating on the growth-rate selection process, and in terms of perspective planning the author's main concern is to emphasise the need to choose the correct variant, which in practice implies selecting an appropriate growth rate, and to illustrate the costs of an excessive growth rate.

The model contains two basic assumptions: (*a*) growth is supply-determined; and (*b*) the savings rate, the growth of employment rate and the capital-output ratio are all centrally determined. In the initial stages of perspective-plan construction the planner draws a rough plan outline assuming a rate of growth which is above the rates achieved in the past and imputes some hypothetical capital-output ratio coefficient. Thus

$$\Delta Y/Y = [I/Y \times 1/m] + u - a, \qquad (1)$$

where $\Delta Y/Y$ = the rate of growth of output, m = capital-output ratio, u = revenue gained through disembodied technical progress, a = revenue lost due to capital depreciation, and I = gross investment.

Following socialist national income accounting practice, the planner divides total investment into productive investment and unproductive investment. Using the given capital-output coefficient, the annual levels of productive investment and inventories are calculated; the difference between the sum of these two items and total national income determines the sum available for consumption and unproductive investment. Then the planner attempts to determine future levels of consumption using a wide range of data. Having divided the national income into these four components, the planner is able to calculate approximately total domestic demand using production-function data with an allowance for future technological progress. Domestic industry is divided into supply-determined units, that is industries operating with capacity ceilings, and demand-determined units, which are free of such constraints. Demand-determined industries are allotted a planned production level high enough to meet home demands for their products and also to yield an export surplus large enough to cover in value terms any shortfalls in the supply-determined industries' capacities to meet domestic demands. Achieving balance-of-payments equilibrium in practice may prove very difficult, and foreign demand, together with labour supply, could become major constraints on the plan and its implied rate of growth. The planner is now able to re-estimate the total amount of productive investment required, subject to possible foreign-trade and labour constraints. This level, however, may still prove to be too high due to its impact on consumption and unproductive investment, in which case the rate of growth of the economy will have to be further reduced [45,46,47].

THE MATHEMATICAL APPROACH TO PLANNING

In the post-Stalin era (after 1953), two major issues were at stake: (*a*) whose preferences should dominate the system and determine the goals of long-run development; and (*b*) the problem of the efficiency of the traditional planning system in fulfilling these goals. The first issue was never debated and the centre's preferences remained dominant. In an attempt to tackle the second issue research into mathematical economic theory and planning was officially revived in the Soviet Union. The mathematical approach included the increased use of the linear-programming technique. This method when applied to resource allocation consists of the optimisation of an objective function, given some resource-feasibility contraints and the available set of production techniques. It was observed that any linear-programming solution reveals a set of dual variables which are equivalent to 'embedded' shadow prices (resource opportunity costs). These optimal prices can then serve as a check on the efficiency of plan allocations. Thus a solution to both the resource-allocation and valuation problems would be possible. It was also noted that the efficiency prices were conceptually independent of the type (i.e. socialist or capitalist) of economic system operating.

The first area of Soviet planning doctrine to be subjected to a mathematic approach was that of inter-industry or input-output analysis. A major problem for the centre is the potential incompatibility of its planning decisions. A decision to plan for a certain output of some priority good will involve economy-wide ramifications in terms of increased outputs of other goods used as inputs in the priority good's production process. A chain-reaction process is stimulated. Thus the planners have to strive for plan consistency, and this is where input-output analysis is useful. The method involves the construction of a transactions table which shows how the output of each industry is distributed to other industries and sectors of the economy, showing also the inputs received by each industry. After a promising start in the 1920s, Soviet work in this field became rather unsophisticated and limited under Stalin's regime, practical planning being conducted with the aid of the so-called 'balance' technique. This technique never attained the theoretical objective of planning consistency, basically because the balances never evolved into an economy-wide network under the 'leading links' method of planning, and also because of the lack of computation techniques and equipment.

During the 1950s Soviet planners returned to the much more refined method of input-output analysis, developed and extended in the United States by Leontief. The Leontief apparatus, plus increasing computer capacities, allowed the Soviet planners to change their methodological approach to plan construction, adopting methods similar to French 'demand-side' planning. The Soviet Union began building computers in 1949, the first commercially available computers being produced in 1955. By 1973 all the European socialist countries except Rumania had begun producing integrated circuit computers. However, it is probably true to say that after a late start, as compared with the West, the socialist countries have failed to make up the lost ground. It was estimated in 1970 that the socialist countries were six to twelve years behind Western Europe in the computerisation of their economies (see Wilczynski [48] and [28] ch. 17).

Zauberman [49] points out that technically the linear

input-output system is but a particular case of the linear-programming system. The former is used to deal with the problems of plan consistency; it enables the planner to compute a set of feasible plan variants. Linear programming has a wider significance and can be used to attack the efficiency problem, its central aim being the construction of an optimal plan. The first Soviet attempt at programming had actually been made by Kantorovich in the 1930s when working on a practical planning problem in the plywood industry. It was not until the 1950s, however, that the over-all importance of the technique for the economy was recognised. The traditional planning methods had proved incapable of producing a single consistent and feasible plan, let alone a set of plan variants ultimately yielding the optimal plan. During the last three decades a great deal of work has been carried out in the Soviet Union in the general area of programming models and the creation of an economic system controlled with shadow prices, Kantorovich and Novozhilov being prominent.

The theory of the optimally functioning socialist economy was developed and continues to be refined by the T.S.E.M.I. (Central Economic Mathematical Institute of the Academy of Sciences). established in 1963. The major ideas for the theory have come from the linear-programming technique and also from systems engineering, the latter yielding the concept of the economy as a complex hierarchical decision-making and planning system. Some writers, such as Keizer [14] and Wiles [50], see the optimal planning school as advocates of centralism and concentration. Ellman [51] and Nove [52] reject this view and point out that the optimal planners advocate a synthesised plan-market system with the centre regulating many areas of the economy through the use of indirect economic instruments, plus a general absence of current planning, and increased reliance on market forces.

Since the late 1950s socialist mathematical planners have increasingly assimilated some of the theoretical principles of cybernetics into their planning theory and practice.

Cybernetics is the science of communication, control and self-regulation within organised systems. Cybernetic systems are dynamic and automatically self-regulating systems [53, 54, 55]. Soviet cyberneticists, mainly computer and operational research specialists co-ordinated by the state committee, *Gostekhnika*, are attempting to work towards the goal of a controlled and automatically self-regulating national economic system, the O.G.A.S. The aim is to create a homeostatic system based on state domination of the economy and operated through a nationwide system of computers. The cybernetic planning model would be fully centralised and concentrated, thus eliminating a basic weakness of the traditional planning mode, which lacked an adequate feedback control mechanism. This weakness often led to unrealistic centrally determined plans and various undesirable practices by enterprises attempting to fulfil plan targets (see Chapter 3). Optimal plans in the cybernetic system would be calculated electronically in physical terms. However, the mathematical economists of the T.S.E.M.I. are opposed to this particular view of an optimally planned economy, and, as we have seen, stress the role of the market and value relations combined with planning.

These are a number of obstacles to the practical implementation of these mathematical planning techniques. The size of any realistic macro model itself presents severe problems. This 'dimensions' problem has been tackled by the development of multi-level programming models based on the Dantzig and Wolfe decomposition principle. Decomposition involves dividing up the economy into units controlled by some over-all co-ordinator. Plan information flows up and down the system, an optimal plan eventually emerging after an iterative process of information exchange (see [41] ch. 3). In cybernetic terms a type of feedback control system, 'simultaneous planning from below and from above', is established. Typical of these multi-level planning systems are the Soviet models of Volkonsky and Pugachev and the Hungarian model of Kornai and Liptak [16]. All three models would make use of the proposed cybernetic nationwide computer network, and while formalising the traditional directive planning system, can also operate with a measure of decentralisation, thus utilising a 'socialist market' mechanism. None of these models has as yet provided a practical solution to the problem of plan size, the proposed iterative procedures being costly and slow to yield the optimal value of the objective function.

Cybernation of the economy also involves unprecedented problems of organising and processing information flows. Work on developing national integrated systems of information has not achieved much in the way of practical results. Kornai sees the planning system as a process of information flows leading to approximate decisions and mutual adjustments between planning levels. Perspective planning in his terms becomes a process of perception, of gathering and evaluating information about the future, the aim being to co-ordinate otherwise independent and often conflicting economic activities [56]. The period of time needed to construct the plan Kornai calls the 'plan-elaboration period'. It is assumed at the beginning of this period that some 'aspiration level' exists, that is to say, that the decision-maker has some tentative and hopefully feasible targets in mind. During the plan-elaboration period the planners attempt to explore as many feasible plan alternatives as possible. The better the planning techniques, the more likely it is that most of the many possible feasible plan variants will be examined. If the original 'aspiration level' falls outside this set of feasible and explored plans, then the decision-maker will have to adjust his original targets. There will probably be a set of politically acceptable alternatives to which the original targets can be adjusted. Thus the process of plan elaboration can be viewed as a process of mutual adjustment until the set of acceptable alternatives overlaps with the set of feasible and explored plans, yielding a set of eligible plan alternatives from which the decision-maker chooses.

Mathematical techniques allow the planners to explore a larger number of feasible plan alternatives and also, Kornai argues, brings home to the decision-makers the opportunity costs involved in choosing between plan variants. This last point highlights another drawback to the use of the programming models, the fact that they all assume that a quantifiable objective function governing the decisions of, say, the Soviet leadership does exist. Keizer [14] takes the view that the objective function does indeed theoretically exist but it is inherently not fully quantifiable. Kornai argues that in the real world the wishes, desires and goals of the political decision-makers are not clear or well-defined before the plan-elaboration period, but that mathematical techniques can act as a sort of learning process allowing decision-makers to order their preferences more consistently. Thus Kornai, and for that matter even Kantorovich, doubt the idea of the uniqueness of the optimal plan, the achievement of some grand over-all solution. The decision-makers in fact should choose from a whole set of eligible plan alternatives which are close to optimum. The actual choice will then be determined by factors that exist but are inherently non-quantifiable and therefore not included in the formal objective function. Taking a pragmatic approach, programming models should be used to provide partial solutions, not the over-all solution to the national plan. Mathetical planning can also act as a link between the immensely complex empirical economic system and the limited perceptive capabilities of human political decision-makers. It allows a vast amount of information to be concentrated into more manageable proportions, thus easing the decision-making task.

Kornai's arguments amount to a refution of both the Lange-type 'market socialist' system and the highly centralised and concentrated directive system achieved through computerisation. His solution to the problem of steering the national economy seems to be a complex synthesis of state planning, the utilisation of mathematical techniques and the selective use of the market mechanism, the combined activity of these two complementary control sub-systems being necessary for a satisfactory control of the over-all economy. The closest his ideas seem to have come to actual planning practice is in the operation of the 'guided market' system in Hungary.

On practical grounds Zauberman and others doubt the workability of this plan-market in the context of a socialist planned economy. Indeed the increased use of programming models itself throws up a number of political problems for the various socialist ruling elites. The models do not allow the same flexibility to the centre that the traditional planning methods do, and, furthermore, the implied switch in methodological approach to demand-side planning could raise the issue of consumers' demands to a politically unacceptable level.

3 Socialist Planning in Practice

THE EVOLUTION OF SOCIALIST ECONOMIC PLANNING

Soviet planning evolved pragmatically in piecemeal fashion, but despite this it is possible to distinguish various phases of development. Tenative steps were taken towards the formulation of a perspective plan around 1920-1, and by 1925 the idea of a planning system utilising three basic time horizons had taken shape. The system combined together: fifteen- to twenty-year plans which were primarily concerned with long-term problems of macro structural change; medium-term plans, usually five-year plans, concerned basically with investment decisions; and finally short-term operational plans, twelve-, six- or three-month plans, concerned with detailed technical, industrial and financial problems, each enterprise receiving its so-called *tekhpromfinplan*. Since 1963 'rolling' five-year plans have been in operation with the major objectives for the end of the fifth year being re-examined each year, the aim being the anticipation of successive stages in investment projects.

Gosplan, the state planning commission, was established in 1921 and given an advisory role until 1928, when its guideline planning calculations, the 'control figures', were used as concrete directives for the first five-year plan (1928-32). This plan marks the birth of the traditional directive planning system that operated in the Soviet Union until the mid-1960s and that was forced on the Eastern European satellite economies in the late 1940s. Then in the 1960s came the establishment of the T.S.E.M.I. and the extension of research work on mathematical planning in the Soviet Union and, on a wider scale, in Eastern Europe. The latter area also saw the first practical attempts at constructing decentralised plan-market systems, beginning in 1954 in Yugoslavia.

The traditional Soviet system was a rigid hierarchical planning and management structure with instructions passing vertically down the system from superior authorities to the enterprises. These directives were commands enforceable by law and accompanied by a system of penalties and incentives to ensure fulfilment or overfulfilment of quantitative plan targets. Under the influence of the 'leading links' method of planning, each five-year plan has concentrated investment resources on particular priority industries or sectors—heavy industry, the energy industries and chemicals (see [25] ch. 5). The simultaneously created buffer sectors have consistently been household consumption, agriculture and, to some extent, infrastructure. The traditional system in its 'ideal' form could operate as a cybernetic system, the economy being governed by the centrally determined plan and feedback mechanisms channelling information on productive capacities, resource availability and plan fulfilment vertically back up the system.

In practice, however, the system has run into a wide range of breakdowns and inefficiences. The economic information provided by the Soviet system has been described as insufficient, inaccurate, irrelevant and slow, the system itself proving extremely costly. Thus the plan construction and implementation system was severely hampered by informational inadequacies [53]. Consequently the system has been 'reformed' a number of times since its inception in 1928. Some of the reforms have been concerned with streamlining the original administrative structure of the system. Three separate structures can be identified: the ministerial system (1928-57), the Sovnarkhozy system (1957-65) and the 'flexible' ministerial system (post-1965). In effect each system has incorporated some basic elements of the others. Other reforms have dealt with the content, quantity and form of the directives issued and the re-examination of identifying the feedback mechanisms (see Spulber [54] ch. 1). By the early 1960s a growing body of opinion in the socialist countries had recognised that the socialist economies had entered a new intensive phase of development and that to meet these new conditions radical economic reforms were needed as part of a movement away from the traditional centralised and concentrated system to a more decentralised and parametrically deconcentrated structure, several East European economists going as far as advocating a synthesised plan and market structure [57].

THE ECONOMIC ADMINISTRATION OF THE SOVIET PLANNING SYSTEM

The 'ideal' version of the traditional system of concentrated centralism requires an all-knowing supreme planner capable of taking vast numbers of optimal decisions and possessing a vast and efficient information network. No one institution, including *Gosplan,* can perform this role for the centre and thus the centre directs the economy through the medium of a number of specific institutions. Detailed decision-making tasks have to be delegated to subordinate agencies through a process of administrative deconcentration, the result being a hierarchical administrative network whose prime function is to improve the efficiency of the planning system. In fact an extremely complicated administrative pyramid was evolved in the Soviet Union. At the bottom of the present planning pyramid are the plan executants, the enterprises which are administered by different levels in the hierarchy. Some enterprises are controlled by the intermediate levels, economic ministries and their departments, other 'special' enterprises in the nuclear and space fields are directly controlled by the Council of Ministers, while some local enterprises are administered by local Soviets (party bodies). Alongside the administrative levels there are planning committees and a territorially organised system of party bodies in the pyramid.

The Soviet administrative system has been based on three technical principles—functional, branch, or sectoral, and territorial. In general terms the sectoral principle dominated in the period 1928-57, the era of the ministerial system, each ministry taking charge of a particular branch of industry. The ministry itself was subdivided into a number of departments according to the functional principle, organising its own material supplies, labour, and so on. Most of the ministries were All-Union, in the sense that they controlled their enterprise from the centre, although some ministries in secondary branches were Union-Republican. Each ministry operated through a system of centralised agencies (*glavki*) which corresponded to sectoral or territorial sub-departments. The number of ministries was increased over time as the economy matured and fairly serious co-ordination problems emerged. There was an increasing tendency towards ministerial self-sufficiency and 'empire-building' tactics. A ministry would set up its own vertically organised national supply system because of the general uncertainty of supplies. This excessive 'departmentalism' led to inefficiencies like excessive transport costs, wastage in the utilisation of by products and a general neglect of regional development.

In an attempt to improve the efficiency of the over-all administrative network, the Sovnarkhozy system, based on the territorial principle, was introduced in 1957. Thirty economic ministries were abolished and 104 regions of administration and regional executive agencies were created. This territorial system officially operated until 1965 but in principle it never evolved into a fully fledged process of territorial deconcentration. Nine of the old economic ministries had been retained and in 1962 steps were taken to reintroduce a sectoral-type administration, with the establishment of the Supreme Economic Council at the All-Union level to direct and co-ordinate the system. In fact the diluted territorial system proved less efficient than the old ministerial system, 'localism' replaced 'departmentalism', co-ordination did not improve significantly, with the bureaucracy continuing to increase.

In 1965 there was a partial return to the sectoral principle of administration when a new system of 'flexible' ministries was established. The new ministries had more duties but less power than their predecessors; in particular they were not responsible for material supplies, this function being reallocated to a new state committee (*Gossnab*) for material/technical supplies, although by 1970 only twenty-four ministries had relinquished control over material supplies. The post-1965 system, despite emphasising the sectoral principle, has retained republican planning agencies and increased their powers; investment policy in particular was to be influenced at the Union-Republican level. The 1965 reform also provided for the grouping of enterprises into production associations, *obedineniia*, but little was done in the 1960s to implement this provision. Since 1970 the Soviet leaders have shown renewed interest in some sort of industrial-concentration movement and in 1973 seemed to be favouring the East German 'industrial association' scheme in which firms are compulsorily grouped together under the control of the association see [24,58,59,60].

THE PLANNING PROCESS

The national economic plan is a co-ordinated programme of action and a 'general perspective', a combination of statistical information, forecasts and concrete directives concerning levels of output and capital formation. The plan, however, does not constitute an end in itself since any process of planned management of the national economy includes, besides plan construction, a mechanism for plan implementation [61]. So far we have distinguished between types of plans on the grounds of time horizons but Zielinski [62] argues that this particular criterion is unsatisfactory and suggests that plans should be distinguished according to the type of data used in their construction. When statistical data are being utilised we are in the realm of perspective planning. These data are the result of mathematical calculations and are derived from given information subject to a range of constraints; the data does not express concrete individual tasks for the plan executants but merely represents a generalised forecast of the desired and probable development of the national economy. In contrast, operative plans are based on data that are the result of a process of aggregation of detailed figures and are expressed as concrete tasks given to plan executants within definite time horizons. In perspective planning there is no necessarily definite time horizon although a period of fifteen to twenty years is usually stipulated on account of extrapolation constraints.

Perspective plans are the responsibility of specialised departments within the state planning commission while operative plans are constructed by the entire planning system from the plan executants through the intermediate bodies and the planning commission to the centre itself. In perfect conditions the Soviet annual planning procedure operates with a continuous interchange of information between the various levels of the planning pyramid until macro magnitudes have been disaggregated down to the enterprise level and the *tekhpromfinplans* completed. Various planning stages can be identified. In the pre-plan stage planners build up a statistical picture (the achievement balance) of the year preceding the 'planned' year. In practice problems occur due to the non-comprehensiveness of Soviet statistics and delays in the communication of planning information. The planning process enters a new stage with the announcement by the centre of the general economic objectives for the coming year and the construction by *Gosplan* of a set of preliminary guideline indicators, 'control figures', which are sent down the planning pyramid to the enterprises. In the next stage information comes back up the hierarchy from the enterprises; each enterprise knows roughly its output target for the planned year, calculates its input needs (claims) using the officially laid-down input norms. The ministries then amend the sector's draft plan in the light of the central directives and the enterprise's claims. At this stage it is important to note a basic characteristic of the Soviet system, the constant 'pressure' applied from above to reduce enterprises' claims and the conflicting tendency for enterprises to overstate input requirements and create safety margins, thereby making plan fulfilment easier. Thus a sort of bargaining process takes place between superior and subordinate organs in the planning system [63]. The planning process enters a further stage when *Gosplan* combines the plan information gathered by the various ministries and its own draft plan and attempts to work out the internal balance of the national plan. Using the balance technique the planners try to reconcile both the demand and supply requirements for the priority products. Two final stages can be distinguished—the first in which *Gosplan* sends the draft national plan to the Council of Ministers for official confirmation, and the second when the confirmed plan is transmitted down the hierarchy and disaggregated to enterprise level.

The use of monetary categories such as prices, wages and credit completes the planning process; financial plans are remitted back to the Finance Ministry and the banking system and the All-Union financial plan is constructed. Financial planning, however, plays an entirely subordinate role, the aim being to adjust monetary to real plans, to determine the value of marketed output and the income and expenditure patterns of the population in the planning period. Monetary and financial flows are planned with the aid of value balances generally expressed in current prices. Three main value balances are constructed—the balances of total product and national income, the balances of receipts and expenditure of the main spending agents, and, lastly, bank balances.

THE TECHNIQUES OF PLANNING

Since all economies face scarcity of resources, achieving a rational allocation of resources is a universal problem. Within this context the Soviet planning system is faced with the twin problems of the consistency and the efficiency of the national plan. The plan should be consistent spatially, thus eliminating any contradictions between national, regional, sectoral or enterprise planning targets, and it should also be consistent in time, with operational, medium and perspective plans forming a coherent system. In practice sectoral planning has been badly co-ordinated, and until 1968 there were a number of different classifications of industrial sectors. The annual operational plan does not include a well-formulated sectoral and regional development strategy. Each territorial unit has a plan but it is merely an aggregation of sectoral and functional plans applying to that particular area. Furthermore, central investment planners often find themselves subject to political pressure from local officials regarding the siting of major new projects. A concern for consistency should also be accompanied by concern for an efficient distribution of scarce resources among different economic activities so that the resultant plan satisfies the preferences of the system's economic sovereign to the highest possible degree.

The technique developed by socialist planners to try and meet the consistency requirement is the balance method, the aim being to arrive at the planned balance of the national economy [64]. The balance presents in table form the availability of resources and the planned allocation of those resources, these two sides of the balance being necessarily in equilibrium. The plan should be consistent at the micro level, thus ensuring that no enterprise has a non-feasible plan, and at the macro level ensuring that total planned requirements match resource availabilities [65].

The traditional balancing method used three groups of balances. First, material balances, which were established for the main industrial and agricultural branches and expressed in kind. Using the notation of modern input-output analysis, a material balance can be written out in the following way: let Xi = total supply of a good i, xij = intermediate input (inter-branch flow into industry j) and Yi = amount available for final demand. The planners need to achieve the equality, $Xi = (xij + Yi)$.

Available resources			*Planned allocation*
Production Imports Stocks with suppliers at beginning of planned period	*Xi*	*xij*	Production needs Inputs into other sectors
		Yi	Free-market allocation State reserves Exports

Thus on the macroeconomic level, if there are n industries the following is true for each of them:

$$X_i = \sum_{j=1}^{n} (x_{ij} + Y_i), \qquad i = 1, 2, \ldots, n.$$

Second, labour balances were drawn up illustrating the sectoral distribution of the labour force. Third, a number of synthetic balances were constructed in monetary units, including the national income balance and an array of financial balances. The over-all national balance, the general synthetic balance, thus provides information on the usage of the total national resources and is calculated in value terms except for manpower.

It is however, important to realise that the plan never got balanced in reality and that during a planning year the demand and supply sides were in fact equated by considerable changes in plan targets and through the operation of the priority principle. Planning consistency was hindered by a lack of reliable data concerning: enterprise production capacities; the time constraint on the processing of the data; a 'dimensions' problem; and finally the uncertain central supply system. Whenever an imbalance appeared in a given sector, *Gosplan* could resort to a range of adjustment processes to strike the balance. To take just two examples, it would examine technological coefficients, the supply norms, for material inputs to make sure that the norms were set at an adequate level, and, if not, would seek to reduce them in selected sectors. The supply norm can be expressed in the following way: to produce some output Xj in branch j it is estimated that x units of output from branch i are needed and so the coefficient of production is

$$\frac{x_{ij}}{X_j}, \qquad i, j = 1, 2, \ldots, n.$$

The final demand for the products of the sector in question could be cut but if the sector is a priority sector then resources would be diverted to it from some buffer sector. The first course of action was difficult to implement because of the 'pressure' exerted by the centre on the economy in the form of 'taut' plans. The second alternative would obviously cause a chain-reaction effect on other sectors' balances. Unfortunately the traditional balance technique took little account of any possible inter-sectoral movements caused by modifications in the original plan.

Montias[66] argues that in the early planning years the balance method had a certain rationale, given the underdeveloped state of the economy and the growth strategy adopted. Nevertheless, as the Soviet economy became more complex and alternative production processes multiplied, the traditional balance method became more and more cumbersome and time-consuming to operate [67]. Consequently, in 1958, work began on the formulation of a more sophisticated planning technique, the method of inter-branch balances, extending work originally carried out in the 1920s. This technique can best be described as input-output analysis. A square matrix of inter-branch balances states what each productive branch supplies to and receives from the rest of the economy; it is a double-entry table. The destination of the output of each industry is found by reading horizontally across the rows and the origin of inputs can be found by reading vertically down the columns [68] (see Table 2).

Using Table 2 it is possible to calculate the total use of intermediate goods from different branches in the production of a given branch, as well as the required total expansion of output in all branches as the result of an increase in the planned output of any one industry. Theoretically, then, the technique will yield a consistent

TABLE 2

Producing branches (i)		Receiving branches (j): Inter-branch flows 1, 2, . . . , n	Total	Final demand accumulation + consumption	Total output
Industry	1	$x_{11} + x_{12}, \ldots, x_{1n}$	x_1	Y_1	x_1
	2	$x_{21} + x_{22}, \ldots, x_{2n}$	x_2	Y_2	x_2
	⋮	Quadrant A	⋮	Quadrant B	⋮
	n	$x_{n1} + x_{n2}, \ldots, x_{nn}$	x_n	Y_n	x_n
Total material costs		$C_1 + C_2, \ldots, C_n$			
Personal income (wages, profits)		$P_1 + P_2, \ldots, P_n$		P	
Surplus product		$S_1 + S_2, \ldots, S_n$ Quadrant C		S Quadrant D	
Total output		$X_1 + X_2, \ldots, X_n$			

x = inter-industry sales.
Y = final demands.
X = total (gross) output.

plan. Using quadrants A and B, and assuming for the sake of simplicity that we are only interested in getting two branches of industry (1 and 2) into a consistent relationship, the following picture emerges:

i \ j	Branch 1		Branch 2		Final demand		Total
Branch 1	x_{11}	+	x_{12}	+	Y_1	=	X_1
Branch 2	x_{21}	+	x_{22}	+	Y_2	=	X_2

It is possible to calculate the quantity of output from industry 1 required for one unit of production from industry 2. The intersection of a row and a column gives the use by one branch of industry j of the production of another branch i in the form of a number x_{ij}; thus, as the total product of the branch is given (Xj), the input-output coefficients of direct requirements, a_{ij}, can be calculated, so that $x_{11}/X_1 = a_{11}$, $x_{21}/X_1 = a_{21}$, and so on.

i	*j* Branch 1		Branch 2		Final demand		Total
Branch 1	$X_1 a_{11}$	+	$X_2 a_{12}$	+	Y_1	=	X_1
Branch 2	$X_1 a_{21}$	+	$X_2 a_{22}$	+	Y_2	=	X_2

In practice there are two ways of calculating the total requirement of intermediate goods from different branches in the production of a given branch: the 'step by step', iterative, method which uses the input-output coefficients of direct rqquirements to establish coefficients of indirect requirements; and second the method which enables the coefficients of total requirements, direct and indirect, to be calculated by matrix inversion [69,70].

There is no doubt that this type of input-output analysis could be widely applied to improve socialist planning practice. Ellman [65] argues that the input-output tool should be used at lower levels in the planning hierarchy to plan the relations between branches of industry. In terms of spatial consistency it forms a link between plans for the basic macro indices and the sectoral and regional plans. In fact the technique has been used mainly in an *ex post* accounting role, estimated balances being restricted to an auxiliary plan-verification role. There are a number of practical difficulties associated with the use of this technique. A complete and detailed table requires a vast amount of statistical and planning information, while the collection of such data is a time-consuming and expensive business. Furthermore, the table depicts 'pure' branches which often do not correspond to their real-world administrative equivalents. Third, aggregation problems frequently cause distortions. Finally, there is the problem of the dichotomy between models in value terms and models in physical units. Models in physical units have advantages for

Soviet planners since they represent a fairly smooth transition from the material balance method. The most important limitation of such an approach is that models in physical units cannot cover the entire range of commodities produced. Theoretically, models in value terms, combined with national income accounts, provide a superior method; in practice the shortcomings of the Soviet price system severely limits the usefulness of value models.

The use of the inter-branch technique does offer the possibility of constructing a number of balanced plan variants instead of the often poorly balanced and frequently late single plan variants which was all that was possible using traditional planning methods. However, the former technique cannot ensure a rational plan and does not guarantee an optimally functioning planning system. As we have seen, the problem of optimisation can be dealt with, in theory, using linear programming, the theory of cybernetics and a national computer network.

At the operational level the mathematical planners of the T.S.E.M.I., for instance, have made a number of practical contributions to improving the Soviet planning system. Apart from the field of variant calculations of the structure of production in medium-term planning, optimisation procedures have been limited to particular sectors of the economy. Production scheduling has been improved, for example, in the Soviet steel industry, the efficiency of investment planning in general has been raised and improvements made in the calculation of fuel costs in the Soviet electricity industry [51].

The advent of this programming approach to planning and the application of input-output analysis have led to a trend in socialist planning methodology away from the traditional 'resource' planning approach towards demand planning and the problem of how to plan final consumption in long-term planning models. Under the traditional planning system the consumption sector was accorded a low-priority, buffer status. Sellers' market conditions were created, noted for the excess of demand over supply at the existing controlled prices. The paradoxical situation emerged of shortages and bottlenecks existing side by side with vast stocks of unsold good which consumers had refused to buy. With the new methodological approach, information about the volume and structure of consumption over a period of fifteen years is required. Further a solution was needed to the crucial problem of what quantifiable objective function expressing consumer demand to use. In the Soviet Union, debates took place over the possibility and propriety of establishing physical consumption targets by 'scientific substantiation' rather than through budget studies, income elasticities and mathematical models of consumer demand [71,72].

The national economic plan in each socialist country now has a counterpart research and development plan for each level of economic administration. A great deal of importance is attached to this structural planning approach, the intention being to promote technologically progressive branches of industry and to combat the tendency for sectional interests to divert economic policy from its optimal course. Wilczynski [48] also sees these plans performing a subsidiary market-research role for the centre.

ECONOMIC REFORMS

By the early 1960s a large number of economists were agreed that the traditional planning system needed radical economic reform, involving a basic shift of emphasis away from a centralised and concentrated structure towards a decentralised and parametrically deconcentrated system. The expanding mathematical planning methodology threw up a number of proposals for 'mixed' plan and market models. Under socialism the market mechanism is superseded in varying degrees by planning, but even in the Soviet Union markets never completely disappeared. Three basic arguments were put forward in favour of an extension of the role of the market in a planned economy. In the first place, a market mechanism is necessary to verify and correct erroneous planning decisions. Second, the market can provide a competitive environment making suppliers more responsive to the needs of buyers. Finally, the efficiency of the directive planning system was weakest at the microeconomic level, because of enterprise *X*-inefficiency problems. Due to inconsistent plans, frequent plan modifications and an unreliable central supply system [73], the Soviet enterprise worked in conditions of uncertainty. (See Wilczynski [74] for a survey of risk and uncertainty in socialist economies and the impact of the economic reforms on the problem of risk.) This situation was aggravated by the practice of 'taut' planning, the centre pressurising the economy by deliberately setting and striving for very ambitious yearly plan targets. In order to ensure that the goods produced conformed to their specific preferences, the centre imposed numerous performance criteria or 'success indicators' on the enterprises. The prime indicator, gross output, was buttressed by a number of other critieria, covering labour productivity, cost reductions, and so on. Enterprises were encouraged to make profits, but up until 1965 profit did not serve as a major success criterion [75,76]. The enterprise's reaction to this type of economic environment was to strive for as 'slack' a plan as possible, the enterprise manager's main concern being to create a safety margin in the form of an 'easy' plan target, combined with excessive stock holdings, a lack of innovation and general inertia. A complicated incentive system was tied to the performance criteria but the 'bonus' system only served further to encourage the enterprise to aim for slack plans. The value of the bonus depended on fulfilment or overfulfilment of the planned target. However, due to the practice of 'planning from the achieved level', overfulfilment of this year's target meant a higher target next year, while failure to meet the target meant no bonus at all. (For a contrary view and an analysis of allocative inefficiency at higher levels of decision-making; see Abouchar [77] and a critique of that paper by Clark [78].)

There have been economic reforms throughout the socialist bloc, 'conservative' in approach in the 1950s and more radical in the 1960s, but their exact form and influence have varied from country to country. Brada [79] categorises the philosophies underlying the reforms as either 'plan-improving' or 'plan-abolishing'. The reforms have been mainly concerned with the microsphere and the lack of an effective feedback mechanism; their general trend has been towards reducing the number of microeconomic targets in the plan. 'Plan-improving' reforms have generally been based on ideas similar to those put forward by the Soviet economist Liberman in 1962, the Soviet Union itself initiating limited experiments along Liberman lines and in 1965 undertaking some general economic reforms [28]. These reforms were based on the belief that centralised direction of a complex industrial economy is possible and that the efficiency of the directive planning system can be significantly improved merely by changing the incentive system applied to enterprises. This strategy of reform has also been followed to a varying extent by East Germany, Poland, Rumania and Bulgaria. 'Plan-abolishing' reforms, on the other hand, are based on the proposition that centralised planning is not suitable for complex industrial economies and that central control should be limited to the macrosphere, the market mechanism consequently being given a wider role to play in improving economic efficiency. Hungary and Czechoslovakia (1968), following an earlier lead by Yugoslavia, adopted strategies which appeared to embody this point of view. In general it would appear that the process of market parametric deconcentration and increased enterprise autonomy have gone furthest in Hungary and Yugoslavia and least in Rumania and the Soviet Union [21,80,81].

In all the socialist economies, enterprise performance criteria have been altered; instead of gross output, financial indicators, such as sales, profits or profitability in relation to capital, are now being used. In the Soviet Union, for example, three incentive funds for enterprises have been set up out of profits from which bonuses are paid. Detailed planned output and input directives are being supplemented and in some countries replaced by indirect financial 'levers'. The transition from a planning system in which real flows enjoyed absolute priority to one in which account is taken of the fact that monetary flows react upon the real flows has been very gradual. The transition itself has been closely linked with increasing consumer incomes and changing household choice patterns and with an increase in enterprise autonomy. The centralised system of supply has also been partially replaced by wholesale trade through indirect horizontal contacts between enterprises; and finally a charge for the use of invested capital has been introduced.

Nevertheless, 'diversity' is the key word in any description of the extent of the reform movements in the socialist economies. In the Soviet Union, intra-industry transactions are not market-type processes; usually bilateral, they are still subject to detailed control by superior administrative authority. The *Gossnab*-controlled supply system remains highly centralised and little has been done to implement direct ties and wholesale trading. Further, as was mentioned in the last chapter, there has been no radical reform of the Soviet price system, and this affects the dependability of the profit criterion as a guide to efficiency and severely limits any role for market forces. Even in Eastern Europe, only in Yugoslavia do prices in principle operate as a general means of market-type information. In Hungary prices play this role for a limited number of products while the other socialist economies adopt methods similar to those employed in the Soviet Union [82].

The economic reforms instituted in East Germany are typical of the 'plan-reforming' philosophy. The country has retained the basic Soviet system of universal planning as well as assimilating some of the post-1965 Soviet reforms, and at the same time evolved some new organisational features such as the 'industrial association'. The creation of associations was an attempt to change the intermediate levels of the planning hierarchy from the bureaucratically based ministries to the business-based associations. The associations were groupings of enterprises either as vertical trusts or horizontal combines. All the Eastern European economies established their own version of the institution. The official view was that the association was a compromise between maintaining central control and allowing greater enterprise autonomy. In the event the balance of choice between the two functions differed from country to country; in East Germany the association has served as a means of retaining control over enterprise autonomy.

The Hungarian economic reforms of 1968 typify the 'plan-abolishing' philosophy. A guided market system was created, following the Yugoslav road to greater enterprise autonomy and an active market mechanism. The Hungarian enterprise drafts its own annual plan, working through its association, the centre confining its attention to the long-term plan. The price system has been made more flexible through the creation of a three-category system—centrally set 'fixed' prices, 'controlled' prices, that is prices subject to a maxima or other centrally determined limit, and 'free' prices influenced by market conditions. Membership of the association after 1968 was not compulsory and the association itself was intended to be a form of voluntary enterprise co-operation. Unlike the Soviet Union, where investment planning remains highly concentrated, in Eastern Europe there has been a trend towards enterprise (association) autonomy in capital formation. In Hungary, only major investment projects are included in the macroeconomic plan and financed out of the budget. Finance from non-budgetary sources, that is enterprise funds and bank credit, are becoming increasingly important.

In conclusion, it is probably fair to comment that the empirical planning systems in the socialist economies have so far fallen short of the theoretical 'mixed' plan and market systems. (See Zielinski [83,84] for a discussion of the problems of designing a new economic system and of achieving an effective transition from the old to the new system.) As for the future, Zauberman's pessimistic judgement about the unworkability of 'mixed' socialist systems may well be proved valid, as recently, even in Hungary, a number of reconcentration measures have been instituted and a process of 'creeping reconcentration' initiated, a process already evident in the rest of the socialist camp [85].

4 The Theoretical Foundations of Indicative Planning

The purpose of indicative planning is to promote faster and more stable growth and to encourage more efficient investment. Such a plan will contain a forecast or target rate of growth for the economy as a whole, for a specified future time period, and a consistent set of microeconomic forecasts or targets. The planning exercise involves raising the overall level of demand expectations and removing the uncertainty with which expectations are held.

There are two main theories underpinning indicative planning. The 'theory of demand expectations' is a theory of growth. The 'theory of indicative planning' is concerned with the problem uncertainty.

THE 'THEORY OF INDICATIVE PLANNING'

The development of the theory of indicative planning owes much to Massé, who has pointed out that planning in practice (in France) preceded the theory [86]. The theory of 'pure' indicative planning, as originally developed by Massé, related to the 'liberal' period of French planning of the late 1950s and early 1960s (see Chapter 5). A complementary relationship between the plan and the market economy is postulated. The existence of market failures, conventionally dealt with by government action (see Chapter 1), is referred to, but it is argued that the basic defect of the price system is its failure to cope with the efficiency problem caused by the fact that private decision-makers hold different views about the future. The need to render expectations consistent has become more important with faster technological progress. It is necessary to plan investments on longer-term and more accurate forecasts and this requires the co-ordination of forecasts at the national level if bottlenecks and under-utilised capacity are to be avoided. The problem could be solved by a system of forward markets, where contracts were made now for future demands and supplies, but such a set of forward markets does not exist. However, through the collection and exchange of information and by making individual plans 'coherent' (i.e. by removing the inconsistencies between the forward plans of different branches of economic activity), the mere existence of the national plan reduces uncertainty and makes for a more efficient use of resources. The result is achieved essentially through the self-implementing nature of the plan, derived from the persuasive powers of its internal consistency, which induces entrepreneurs to make the appropriate investment decisions. This will be so provided everybody 'plays the game' by making decisions consistent with the forecasts which they have helped to produce.

Lutz [7] has set out a detailed critique of this theory. The criticisms relate partly to the difficulties the French have had in practice, but mainly to its validity as a theory of central planning for the market economy. It is the latter with which we are principally concerned in this chapter. The crucial question raised is whether it is possible to aggregate different individual views into a genuine common view about the future. The advocates of indicative planning have often referred to it as 'market research on a national scale', implying that planning is a logical extension of the forecasting activity of firms and that aggregation can be achieved unambiguously. The argument that Lutz has put forward is that in a competitive economy, under conditions of uncertainty, the plans of firms cannot add up to a national plan. The argument is that, since there is no simple way of summing the individual views (subjective probabilities) held concerning the future, a common view of the future cannot be arrived at. The aggregation problem exists in moving from firms' forecasts to a branch forecast and from branch forecasts to the larger aggregates. It is not only impossible to aggregate beliefs, it is unlikely that beliefs will be perfectly revealed since competition in forecasting is an integral part of competition as a whole. Massé's view implies that the market system would work more efficiently the more perfect is foresight about the future. Lutz's argument is that if perfect foresight or certainty were possible, risk would be eliminated and the market system could not function. If a common view about an uncertain future were achieved, through successful collective forecasting, by the elimination of competition in forecasting, the competitive system would likewise be destroyed. Thus the implications of arriving at a common view about the future, even if this were possible, would be disastrous for the market economy.

It is also argued that it is impossible to disaggregate large aggregates to provide meaningful information at lower levels of aggregation. In particular, merely providing firms with information about future branch output, if that were possible, is insufficient by itself to enable them to predict their share of the market. Lutz based some of her arguments on Richardson's analysis of this problem [87]. Richardson himself has since related his arguments specifically to indicative planning [8].

An argument which Richardson has put forward is that disaggregation is very questionable below the level of the large aggregates such as consumption and investment since disaggregation represents a movement from the more predictable to the less predictable. The conventional argument that an industry's future can be calculated from the rate of growth of national output *via* the calculation of income elasticity of demand is dismissed on the grounds that it is only one of the factors affecting demand for that industry's output and one that becomes less important the faster is the pace of technological progress. The problem of moving from the industry's output to firms' market shares is even greater. One argument advanced is that even if meaningful forecasts were possible for an industry, unless that industry was homogeneous the information would be of little assistance to firms. The argument has two aspects:

first, that more disaggregation is needed, but then the greater the degree of disaggregation, the less credible the forecasts will be; second, there is the empirical question as to whether there are any consistent relationships at the various levels of disaggregation which, even for an homogeneous industry, is recognised by, and would be meaningful to, firms [88].

However, the main argument which Richardson has advanced is that, under perfect competition, market shares are theoretically indeterminate. The argument is that it would not be possible, under conditions of perfect competition, for firms to know how much to produce since the price system does not provide information about the supply plans of competitors; but not only will the distribution of the industry's output be indeterminate, it will also be impossible to arrive at an industry forecast since the latter consists of the aggregation of firms' forecasts. The argument is, then, that perfect competition cannot, even in theory, provide a solution. Nor can the informational deficiencies be remedied by a recontracting system of the Walrasian kind where forward contracts to buy and sell are made consistent *via* an iterative process. The reason advanced for this is the imperfection of knowledge. A consistent set of forward contracts is unobtainable because consumers cannot predict their future needs and producers cannot predict future production possibilities. Since the indicative planning process is based on the logic of Walrasian *tatonnement* (the iteration to equilibrium), it cannot provide a means of welding individual expectations into a national plan.

The main conclusion that emerges from the critique of the pure theory of indicative planning is that individual expectations cannot be combined into a common view as represented in a national plan. Therefore indicative planning as planning for the market economy is logically invalid. The view taken is that, rather than try to consolidate expectations into a common view, it is preferable that decisions about the uncertain future be made on the basis of a plurality of views.

A sophisticated version of the pure theory of ideal indicative planning has been developed by Meade [9] which meets the major criticisms made of Massé's version. However, before discussing Meade's contribution, a number of preliminary points may be made about some of the arguments outlined so far. It should be noted that the position which Massé has taken on the issue of market shares is that planning should not be disaggregated from the branch to the firm level because this is where flexibility and risk play their role. Moreover, the view of perfect competition taken by Richardson, involving the indeterminancy of market shares, has not been generally accepted. His critique of indicative planning itself is questionable [88]. To argue that the theory of indicative planning cannot rest on the theory of perfect competition does not mean that it cannot have any theoretical foundation at all, and to assert that the level of disaggregation achievable by indicative planning is unhelpful to firms is an empirical question to be proven. On the former point it is noteworthy that Richardson's fellow critic has pointed out that indicative planning does not involve the introduction of universal perfect competition [7].

Lutz has argued, however, that departing from the Walrasian assumption of perfect competition implies that collective forecasting be based on a very complex model which it would be impossible to formulate in practice. One way out of this difficulty is to assume that each industry acts as though it were one firm, that is to say, that a cartel arrangement exists. (The role of cartels in French planning is discussed briefly in Chapter 5). The final point to be made is that the discussion so far relates to pure indicative planning. The original version of Massé's theory of indicative planning, based on the 'liberal' period of French planning of the late 1950s and early 1960s, was reworked by Massé in response to changing conditions in the French economy when French planning took on a 'new look' towards the mid-1960s. The practical and theoretical developments which then took place are considered later (see Chapter 5), but at this point it should be noted that Lutz has argued that the 'new look' involved the virtual abandonment of the co-ordinating function of forecasts and the plan's self-implementation.

Having made these points we now consider Meade's contribution to the pure theory of ideal indicative planning. The crucial point is that everyone in the economy is faced with uncertainty but a distinction must be made between 'market' uncertainty and 'environmental' uncertainty. Market uncertainties are matters about which some decision-makers are fairly certain whilst others are very uncertain, for example producers' lack of knowledge about consumers' demand plans. It is this kind of uncertainty which indicative planning can remove. The uncertainties which Lutz and Richardson wish to preserve are of the environmental kind. Environmental uncertainties are those matters about which all decision-makers are inevitably uncertain, for example exogenous events, like the weather, which affect demands and supplies, or international economic factors which affect the demand for a particular country's exports, and uncertainty about the parameters in consumption and production functions.

The theory is developed on the basis of a number of assumptions which are later relaxed to examine the complications which emerge. The assumptions are as follows: perfect competition throughout the economy; the absence of those factors (externalities, monopoly, and so on), which would call for government action so that the economic function of government is just to organise economic forecasting; the world will last a definite time period so that everyone knows precisely the period covered by the plan; and a demographic assumption implying that the period covered by the plan is relevant to everyone now alive but to nobody else. It may be noted here that when this demographic assumption is dropped, the implication is that forward markets are precluded and the case for indicative planning is manifest. Given these few heroic assumptions the economy can be extremely complicated, including insurance markets. (The relevance of insurance markets, or rather their absence, becomes clear later.)

Meade's argument is that if there are no environmental uncertainties, the information-exchange process of indicative planning (on the assumption that the process is subtle enough to deal with the problem of complementary goods) can mimic the Pareto-optimal results that are generally regarded as obtainable by a comprehensive set of forward markets. Equilibrium prices, which balance supplies and demands at each point of time during the plan, can be forecast and, if individuals' present plans are made on the expectation of these prices (of inputs and outputs), supplies and demands will in fact balance. Thus indicative planning provides a way of removing market uncertainties *ex ante*, thereby avoiding the inefficiencies entailed by *ex post* adjustments. When environmental uncertainties are admitted, the plan would need to take the form of a set of plans so that the various possible environmental paths which the economy could follow are covered. Again, if everyone plays the game, market uncertainties will be eliminated and the results would be an efficient use of resources.

Significantly, it is not necessary for there to be an agreed common view about the probability of each environmental path. Everyone would be free to make, and act on, his own view as to the probability of future environmental changes but uncertainty about market conditions on each environmental path would be removed. However, since producers may insure against each environmental development, they face no risks; but where insurance is ruled out, producers will face risks and their profits will depend upon how good their judgement is about the future.

Many complications emerge when all the simplifying assumptions upon which the pure theory of ideal indicative planning is developed are relaxed. In practice, of course, a very limited number of environmental uncertainties could be considered. Information would be solicited about future behaviour along these representative environmental paths, but if private decision-makers are free to assess the probability of these paths, and to consider the possibility of other paths, there would remain a considerable amount of 'residual uncertainty', that is on the paths not considered in the plan, they would be faced with market as well as environmental uncertainty. But although indicative planning would not then eliminate market uncertainties, it would considerably reduce them since the individual decision-makers could use the information provided for the representative time paths as a bench-mark for making their own forecasts. Even if the planners solicit information about only one single path, the plan could be useful in this way.

There is a further consequence of the existence of a large number of possible time paths. The number of environmental possibilities increases the longer the time period. Relaxing the assumption that the world will last a definite period covered by the plan implies that for practical purposes the time horizon of the plan must be limited. Thus there will be uncertainty about periods beyond the plan. This would mean uncertainty during the plan period, in which market information for periods beyond the plan is relevant to decision-making during the plan period. The implication drawn by Meade is that the plan must be subject to continual extension and revision to take account of new information as it becomes available. This point is also made by Lutz. The burdens on the planning system of regularly revising the plan (rolling planning) would, of course, be enormous.

Another problem is that in practice it would not be possible to formulate a fully comprehensive plan which covered all variables, that is products, consumption demands, and so on, quite apart from covering every environmental possibility. Thus the plan would have to be based on an econometric model of the economy where, for example, output would be broken down only to aggregates such as manufactured products and agricultural products. However, even an aggregate plan of this kind will, according to Meade, reduce some market uncertainties.

When the assumption of perfect competition is relaxed, the theoretical and practical difficulties are compounded [9]. One problem which emerges in this context is that of the unwillingness to reveal information and the possibility that the planning process will encourage collusive agreements, a point stressed by Lutz. This raises the general issue of the relationship between indicative planning and competition. (For a discussion of this, see [89].)

The role of the government so far has simply been to organise the collection and dissemination of information and to remove inconsistencies between forecasts in order to reduce uncertainty and thereby encourage more efficient investment. However, governments act in the economy for a number of reasons (see Chapter 1), and this raises the problem of the relationship between indicative planning and other economic functions of government. In Meade's scheme [90], indicative planning in a dynamic economy finds its place alongside both the government's structural plan to achieve its objectives with respect to matters like the distribution of income and the provision of social services and its short-run stabilisation programmes to supplement the structural plan when unexpected events occur.

Our discussion so far has been concerned with an analysis of the theoretical and practical difficulties associated with the pure form of indicative planning or forecasting. Our conclusion is that a logically valid theory can be built up on a set of restrictive assumptions but considerable complications emerge when these assumptions are relaxed. However, indicative planning is generally regarded as involving more than mere forecasting to reduce market uncertainties; in its 'active' form it constitutes a means of achieving targets through the use of implementation instruments (see [7] and [3]).

THE 'THEORY OF DEMAND EXPECTATIONS'

It is usually assumed that removing inconsistencies through the generation of a common view of the future is facilitated if the rate of growth of the economy is planned *ex ante* and held to be a target to which the government is committed. Lutz has pointed out that this assumption is not strictly necessary to the theory of indicative planning as central forecasting, for which the growth rate for the economy can be treated as a forecast rather than a target. Indeed the theory (of demand expectations) relevant to the role of the global figure is most clearly expounded by Beckerman [91] but not with the intention of setting out the argument for target planning [89]. Nevertheless, some argue that the strongest case that can be made for indicative planning is in terms of its role in raising businessmen's expectations of future demand and not in terms of eliminating uncertainty by a set of consistent micro-economic forecasts [92].

The 'pure' theory of demand expectations would, like the 'pure' theory of indicative planning, imply non-interventionist planning [18]. However, Beckerman's theory of demand expectations indicates that the achievable rate of growth is only partly dependent upon the rate which businessmen expect.

The argument advanced by Beckerman is that the evidence suggests that the different growth rates between advanced market economies result only partly from different rates of employment of the factors of production and that differences in the rate of productivity increase are an important factor. It is contended that demand expectations are particularly important in explaining differences in productivity growth rates. The argument is that expectations affect growth because confident expectations will stimulate a greater effort to expand productive capacity both through a higher rate of investment and through improvements in factor productivity. Because of embodied technical progress, a faster rate of gross capital formation may have an automatically favourable effect on the productivity of net capital formation. If this increased capacity permits the realisation of high demand expectations, so that output is able to expand rapidly, economies of scale will cause productivity per unit of factor input to rise.

It is argued that the factor which is most significant in determining confident expectations, and therefore growth, is the buoyancy of exports. Export buoyancy depends on price and technological competitiveness. An initial competitive advantage, generating a rapid expansion of exports, will facilitate a fast rise in productivity which will perpetuate or increase any initial competitive advantage. This will stimulate investment through a favourable effect on profit margins. Technological progress can accentuate any initial technological lead in products, conferring a competitive advantage not represented in normal price comparisons. Thus there is a 'virtuous-circle' element in the growth process.

The relevance of the theory of demand expectations to indicative planning is clear. The rate of growth may be increased by persuading private decision-makers that faster growth is possible. Thus, although getting a target or forecast rate of growth widely accepted may not, by itself, be sufficient to achieve that rate, capacity will not grow quickly unless expectations about future long-run prospects are changed.

A number of criticisms have been made of this theory. It has been pointed out that the evidence in support of the theory is not overwhelming and that the importance of demand expectations has been exaggerated *vis-a-vis* other factors such as education, managerial efficiency and labour relations [89]. Thus the extent to which reliance should be put on efforts to change expectations is open to dispute.

A number of writers (for example [5,89]) have stressed that supply-side constraints need to be carefully considered when inducing expansion by raising expectations. For example, raising the expectations of those responsible for investment decisions may increase only the demand for capital, and not its supply, and inflation could result unless consumption is held back until production increases enough to provide for faster growth of consumption as well as investment. A difficulty emerges here in that holding back consumption will have the effect of lowering expectations, tending therefore to a reduction in investment. The solution might be to persuade businessmen that higher investment now would be justified because less consumption now implies more consumption later [18]. However, the wide dissemination of the growth ethic associated with indicative planning brings with it high consumption expectations from consumers which are difficult to restrain, and in a fully employed economy with a slowly growing working population, a labour-supply constraint might quickly emerge unless productivity increases rapidly.

The problem of the relationship between a faster rate of economic growth and an influx of imports can be a crucial one in economies with supply-side constraints. The danger is that raising demand expectations in such circumstances would lead to an influx of imports not met quickly enough by an expansion of exports so that the balance of payments runs into deficit [93]. The usual solution adopted to tackle this problem is to slow down the rate of growth through demand-dampening policies so that imports are reduced. An alternative approach has been developed recently by French planners, based on Courbis's theory of the 'competitioned' economy (see [94,95] and Chapter 5). On the assumption that substitutability exists between imports and domestic production in the sectors exposed to international competition, imports can be reduced by increasing output in the exposed sector.

The effect of supply constraints on exports is important. In the theory of demand expectations it is the buoyancy of exports which determines confident expectations, but exports depend in the first place on competitiveness, that is supply-side factors. Clearly, the national plan targets, important as a means of influencing domestic expectations, will have little effect on the external demand for a country's exports [89]. However, as Denton has argued, if policies to act on supply factors to improve the competitiveness of exports are embodied in a comprehensive plan, it may facilitate their acceptance and implementation. The same argument is applicable to all supply-side constraints, not only those constraining exports. For example, just as it is probably easier to mobilise opinion in favour of a specified global target role of growth rather than just 'faster growth', it could be that similar benefits may accrue from packaging a set of policy changes as a co-ordinated programme for the achievement of quantified objectives.

It has been argued that although an indicative plan may generate growth by raising the general level of expectations, it may not be the best way to do so [88]. The argument is that raising demand smoothly and rapidly by monetary and fiscal policy may have a more beneficial effect on expectations than a plan containing a large number of forecasts or targets whose accuracy may be doubted. However, there is an argument, which has been put forward by Harrod, to the effect that indicative planning may be needed in addition to monetary and fiscal policy [5]. If monetary and fiscal policies are used to provide the correct conditions for growth but entrepreneurs do not embark upon expansion because of uncertainty, a problem arises. If monetary and fiscal policies are already earmarked for creating the right conditions for growth (e.g. fiscal policy, ensuring there are sufficient savings to finance the required investment), they cannot be diverged from in order to give entrepreneurs an added stimulus without creating demand inflation. Therefore a further instrument of policy, namely indicative planning, is needed. A similar view has been expressed by Black [4] but an additional point is made. Whereas indicative planning may be used in conjunction with monetary and fiscal policy to secure faster growth, planning is a better means of achieving stable growth and efficient investment. Monetary and fiscal policies used to achieve a stable level of aggregate demand may have adverse effects on the efficient choice of investment projects. Misallocation of resources may occur because contractionary policies may induce abandonment of high-productivity projects, and expansionary policies may induce less-productive projects to be begun without adequate planning. Moreover, even if aggregate demand is stabilised, the allocation of total investment between sectors and projects may still be inefficient because fluctuations in demand in particular sectors may lead to inefficient investment choices being made in response to temporary demand conditions. Thus indicative planning is seen as a better means of achieving stable growth and efficient investment than monetary and fiscal policy.

We may now summarise the conclusions which emerge from our discussion of the theoretical foundations of indicative planning. Indicative planning can, in theory, through its effect on the general level of expectations and through reducing the uncertainty surrounding expectations, promote faster and more stable growth and can encourage more efficient investment. However, it is no easy matter to set up a system of indicative planning which will work well in practice.

5 Indicative Planning in Practice

THE ORIGINS AND DEVELOPMENT OF FRENCH INDICATIVE PLANNING

France, the birth-place of indicative planning, provides the most enduring example of planning for a market economy. In 1976 the Seventh Plan was unveiled with a target rate of growth of 5.5 – 6 per cent p.a. The plan aims to create 1.1 million jobs, to reduce inflation below 6 per cent, to remove the balance-of-payments deficit and to make a number of improvements on the social front. The Sixth Plan (1971-5) was characterised by the sophisticated techniques used in its preparation, the plan itself stressing competitiveness with particular emphasis on industrial growth but also including social objectives. The Fifth Plan (1966-70) was notable for the attempt to introduce value planning (i.e. to reconcile physical and financial flows), the reduction in the number of targets and the introduction of plan-monitoring devices. The Fourth Plan (1962-5) saw the introduction of social-investment and regional-policy objectives, was technically sophisticated and contained considerable detail (in physical targets). It was the Fourth Plan which attracted attention in other West European countries, notably the United Kingdom. The Third Plan (1958-61) can be regarded as the first real attempt at a coherent national economic plan although a step in this direction had taken place in the Second Plan (1954-7), which represented a considerable extension of the plan from the few key sectors of the First (Monnet) Plan. The Monnet Plan covered the early post-war years originally to 1950 but was extended to 1953 and consisted essentially of a set of investment programmes for the basic industries.

Although the origins of French planning may be traced back to the ancient tradition of state intervention [96], the institution of national economic planning after 1945 can be seen as a pragmatic response to the problems of the immediate post-war situation when the task of reconstruction required considerable government intervention. Not only was the economy suffering from the effects of war damage, it still felt the effects of the pre-war depression. Overseas aid was badly needed and the Americans required a clear indication of the uses to which aid would be put. The economic situation and the fact that the political atmosphere was favourable to planning [97] explain the emergence of the planning experiment in France. The form which national economic planning took and the reasons for planning becoming a lasting feature of the French economy, owe much to Jean Monnet [98], who was the first head (*Commissaire General du Plan*) of the General Planning Commissariat (*Commissariat General du Plan* or *C.G.P.*) which was set up in 1946.

Monnet realised that, despite the government's great economic power and the left-wing political ascendancy, which were both manifest in the early post-war nationalisation programme, planning would only work and endure as a collective effort with wide participation in the planning process. Thus Monnet looked beyond the immediate post-war problems and was instrumental in developing the framework for permanent planning. The key concept underlying the approach adopted has been that of the 'pre-concerted economy' (*l'économie concertée*) where an agreed plan has resulted from a process of consultation and information exchange between the parties relevant to the plan [98]. Such planning has been seen as the means whereby businessmen's demand expectations can be raised, the excessive pessimism of French businessmen having been held responsible for slow growth in inter-war France [89], and whereby the uncertainty with which expectations are held can be reduced.

The institutional tools created by Monnet to realise collective planning were the C.G.P. and the Plan (Modernisation) Commissions. The C.G.P. is the key planning instrument in France. It acts as co-ordinator and supervisor of the work done by others in the process of formulating and implementing the plan. The C.G.P. has always been small in size, the senior planners numbering only about fifty (about thirty in 1946). Thus, as befits a central planning office in a market economy, the C.G.P. has avoided looking like a large, all-powerful body with great interventionist powers. Formally, the C.G.P. is not a ministry itself but is attached to the Prime Minister's Office (having been attached to the Minister of Finance between 1952 and 1962). Its role within the central economic administration has been to act as a neutral meeting place where conflicts between ministries can be resolved. The C.G.P., working essentially through the Plan Commissions, has also acted as a meeting place for information exchange and agreement between the administration and the business world.

Despite its small size and non-ministerial position, the C.G.P. has survived and exerted a powerful influence in economic matters. It has succeeded by avoiding making political enemies and by trying to coexist peacefully with the other economic agencies, particularly the Ministry of Finance with whom its relationship has often been uneasy. The heads of the C.G.P. have been men of considerable ability whose political skill has ensured its survival and influence. The role of the C.G.P. and its head has been regarded as a politically neutral one but in recent years there has been a politicisation of planning as the Planning Commissioner has become more an advocate of the government's preferences rather than fulfilling the neutral role of consensus planning [99]. At the institutional level this is reflected in the fact that there is now also a Deputy Minister for the Plan attached to the Prime Minister's Office. In 1974 a Planning Council, chaired by the President and including the Prime Minister, the Financial Minister, the Minister of Labour and the Planning Commissioner, was set up. The Council meets monthly to consider major factors (such as the balance of payments) which affect planning and was instituted to provide a more flexible means of adapting general objectives to current events. The setting up of this new planning body has been interpreted as an indication that the planners are now more closely constrained within political guidelines [100].

The Plan Commissions' primary role has been to assist the C.G.P. in the preparation of the plan. They were conceived by Monnet as the means whereby the planned and the planners can work together to produce an agreed plan, thereby facilitating its self-implementation. The composition of the Plan Commissions reflects this aim. There is no fixed balance of representation (members being appointed on the recommendation of the Planning Commissioner) but their structure is essentially tripartite, consisting of employers, workers and civil servants. It has been argued that the main dialogue has been between the planners and big business, the workers being under-represented [101]. Until 1962 the Commissions were called together each time a new plan was to be prepared and were then dissolved, but since then they have held annual meetings as part of the follow-up procedure for the plan. Their annual reviews of plan implementation provide an indication of what revisions may be necessary.

There are two types of Plan Commission, vertical and horizontal. The former represent sections of economic activity, the latter carry out a general synthesising function. Each Commission sets up working parties to deal with particular aspects of its work. The number of Plan Commissions grew from eight for the First Plan to thirty-two for the Fifth Plan. For the Sixth Plan there were twenty-five Commissions [94], with a reduction in the number of vertical commissions responsible for productive sectors reflecting a desire to improve their effectiveness, and an increase in the number of commissions for social functions reflecting the increased attention paid to social problems. Of the horizontal commissions the most important is the General Economic and Financing (C.E.G.F.), which acts as a forum where more general development aspects are discussed and to which other commissions report.

A summary of the preparation stages of the Sixth Plan illustrates the role of the C.G.P. and the Plan Commissions as well as that of other planning bodies. The preparation took over four years and in total involved more than 5000 people. The preparation stages were three: the administrative, options and plan-specification phases. The first phase began early in 1966 and continued until mid-1969, including a year's delay due to the events of 1968 (for a discussion of which see [101]). This phase provided the framework for the work of the Plan Commissions. The main aspects of this phase were an analysis of the problems involved in the preparation of the Fifth Plan, the use of the physico-financial model (FIFI) to provide the Commissions with a picture of the 1971-5 period, and the undertaking of a programme of long-term studies. The latter have been a feature of French planning since the Third Plan, in order to provide a longer perspective for the medium-term plans, but were given more emphasis in the preparation of the Sixth Plan. The technical work involved in the administrative phase was carried out by the C.G.P. and two divisions of the Ministry of the Economy and Finance (M.E.F.), that is the Forecasting Directorate (D.P.) and the National Institute of Statistics and Economic Research (I.N.S.E.E). The latter acts as a central statistical office and contains considerable economic and econometric expertise upon which the C.G.P. and the M.E.F. are heavily dependent, and was made responsible for running FIFI. The D.P., created in 1965 out of the Economic and Financial Research Department (S.E.E.F), is involved in the preparation of the annual budget, which should provide the link between short- and medium-term forecasting and policy. But attempts to secure the link between the annual budget and the medium-term plan has not been altogether successful [102]. To try to obviate the traditional rivalry between the M.E.F. and the C.G.P., joint Plan-Finance work groups, serviced by the D.P. and I.N.S.E.E., were set up to achieve administrative consensus for the Sixth Plan.

By July 1969 the C.G.P. was ready to report to the government on the problems which had been highlighted by the medium- and long-term studies and asked for orientations for the options phase. During the autumn of

1969 the list of Plan Commission members and their work programme for the options phase were finalised.

The options phase (autumn 1969 to summer 1970) involved the Plan Commissions in a search for solutions to the problems highlighted by the studies of the administrative phase, and the use of FIFI to produce alternative projections (variants) of 1975. By early 1970 the Plan Commissions had drawn up reports from which the C.G.P. drew up a report on the options (5.5, 6.0 and 6.5 per cent p.a.) which was submitted to the government and passed to the Economic and Social Council (E.S.C.). The E.S.C. is a consultative body representing various interest groups which can recommend but not enforce changes [103], The report then went to Parliament for approval, a 5.9 per cent growth rate having been suggested.

The plan-specification phase (autumn 1970 to summer 1971) was the point at which the details of the plan were worked out. The vertical commissions produced detailed branch forecasts on the basis of the options report and suggested how the necessary conditions for their realisation could be created. It has been suggested that the private-sector vertical commissions have acted as cartels in the division of the branch outputs between firms [101]. The horizontal commissions, particularly the C.E.G.F., performed a synthesising function for the work of the vertical commissions. The final outcome was a synthesised plan report prepared by the C.G.P. for transmission to the government. It then went to the E.S.C. and finally to Parliament for approval. Parliamentary approval of the plan has taken the form of accepting the plan as a guide to economic policy and a framework for public investment programmes so that the plan has not been a 'law' in the usual sense of the word [99].

The role of Parliament has become greater in the planning process. Not all plans have been debated in Parliament and it was not until the Fifth Plan that Parliament entered the planning process before its prepartion was complete.

The stages in the preparation process of the Sixth Plan

were essentially the same as those for the Fifth Plan (for a description of which see [7] and for earlier plans see [97, 101, 104]). However, there were some new elements for the Sixth Plan, as evidenced by the restructuring of the Plan Commissions, the greater involvement of the administration (particularly the M.E.F.), the attention paid to long-term studies and the improvement in planning techniques [94].

The method of projection used in earlier plans has been well summarised by Drèze [105], simplified by excluding the foreign sector. From a hypothesis about its rate of growth, a projection of G.N.P. was calculated for the terminal year of the plan. This, when compared with the manpower forecast, gave an indication of productivity changes and allowed investment requirements to be estimated. An aggregate consumption estimate was then obtained by the subtraction of estimated investment and projected public expenditure from G.N.P. On the basis of income elasticities aggregate consumption expenditures were disaggregated into product groups which, together with a breakdown of public expenditure, gave a vector of final demands. Final demands were translated into output and employment estimates for sectors through an input-output matrix.

During the process of plan formulation many adjustments were usually made; for example, as a result of the questionnaire, filled in during the specification phase by the vertical commissions, which provided estimates of sector output, inputs, investment, employment, and so on, the provisional figures for the sectors would be amended. After consistency checks of sector estimates had been carried out, aggregation provided a check on the original aggregate forecasts. A feasible and consistent plan resulted from this process of disaggregation and aggregation.

Until the Sixth Plan the process was therefore carried out in a discretionary manner, adjustments of a subjective kind being made during the iterative process of successive approximation. Discretionary methods are time-consuming and not suitable for working out and comparing more than one growth path. The development of French statistics and of electronic computers has facilitated a move towards a formalised approach using computer-programmed models. FIFI, used in the preparation of the Sixth Plan, is a formalised, computer-programmed model and marked a large step forward in French planning techniques.

The FIFI model is a medium-term projection model of considerable size (approximately 1600 equations) which can carry out projections in volume and value terms simultaneously. In addition to a trend-orientated picture of the economy, based on non-policy changes, to reveal the problems with which the economy would be faced over the plan period, many variants can be considered. FIFI is a simulation model so it can be used to show up the effects on the economy of different policies, thereby illuminating the policy choices needing to be taken to solve the problems facing the economy. Whereas in previous plans objectives were put forward in normative terms, with the policies to achieve them not clearly specified, the FIFI model starts with the policies and compares their consequences with the desired objectives. The model enables not only global but sectoral analyses to be undertaken. Finally, FIFI can be used to synthesise the work of the Plan Commissions.

Although FIFI was the main model used in the preparation of the Sixth Plan it was but one tool amongst many others. It was used in the way outlined above although not all participants in the planning process understood the model or the uses to which it could be put and there was considerable dissatisfaction felt by the participants by the end of the plan-preparation process [94].

Courbis himself [95] and Liggins [94] point out the limitations of the model. It considers the national dimensions and ignores the influence of spatial (regional) factors on national development; financial aspects are not fully integrated; it is limited in detail, distinguishing only seven sectors; the model is static, giving only a picture of the terminal year of the plan and assuming a smooth progression between the base year and terminal year; and the model produces only an economic picture with social variables largely excluded.

The use of a formalised model raised the question of the balance between bigger and better models and wide participation in the planning process. Liggins [94] has observed that in the preparation process over-formalisation was avoided as it was possible to discern the reintroduction of norms and preferences external to FIFI. He has concluded that although improved models are desirable, the case is sound for continuing with open participation in planning.

FIFI is based upon Courbis's theory of the 'competitioned' economy [95]. This is an open economy with unemployment (since competition is insufficient to generate full employment automatically) in which foreign competition is very strong. The theory assumes a competitioned economy containing sectors exposed to strong foreign competition and sectors sheltered from it (or themselves dominantly competitive), a sectoral distinction operational not in the short term but in the medium term. Assuming relatively fixed exchange rates, product prices in the exposed sectors are determined by foreign prices. It is also assumed that substitutability between imports and domestic production exists in the exposed sectors. Because of the price constraint imposed by strong foreign competitors, profits and self-financed investments will be restricted in the exposed sectors. Thus, assuming a relationship between investment and self-financing, output will be adversely affected by foreign competition in the exposed sectors. But assuming that the growth rate of money wages depends on the labour-market situation (the Phillips mechanism), the impact of competition will be countered through wage and cost reductions which come about as a result of the fall in output and employment resultant from an increase in foreign competition. The sectors sheltered from foreign competition (whose output is determined by demand) influence the output of the exposed sectors through the spread of wage and cost changes to the exposed sectors (*via* the Phillips mechanism). However, the output of the exposed sectors is the dominant factor and influences the rest of the economy directly through the demand for intermediate and investment goods and indirectly through the effects of generated incomes on consumption demand. The output of the exposed sectors therefore crucially determines the level of G.N.P., employment and the rate of growth.

In a competitioned economy it is supply, particularly from the exposed sector, and not the level of demand which determines output. Thus action to secure faster growth must concentrate on the supply side and not on the demand side. Hence the stress in the Sixth Plan on competitiveness.

For implementing French plans a wide range of instruments have been used. Masse [3, 86, 98] has stressed the psychological effect of the fact that the planned were involved in preparing the plan. He also attached great importance to the plan's coherence, that is, to the fact that if everyone played the game a balance between supply and demand resulted. Lutz [7] refers to the 'force of persuasion' which the plan thus exerts as the endogenous means of plan self-implementation. But Massé was careful to point out that as well as the psychological factors of implementation, the government had available many practical means of implementing the plan (exogenous instruments in Lutz's terminology). These include general management of the economy and control over the public sector, various specific incentives (fiscal and financial) and contractual agreements with the private sector.

The general instruments (e.g. monetary, budgetary and manpower policies) can be used to regulate the economy in accordance with the general objectives of the plan but the main instruments are of both a short-run and medium-term nature and short-run considerations are often dominant [106]. Direct control over public-sector investment and the monopsonistic power over supplying industries has provided a potentially powerful means of plan implementation. However, in practice it has often even been difficult to persuade the nationalised industries to carry out the plan [101, 107, 108]. Nor has government control over the banking sector been effectively used [109].

Important in the selective financing of both public and private investment have been two agencies in the Treasury division of the M.E.F. They are the Economic and Social Development Fund (F.D.E.S.) and the Deposit and Consignment Office (*Caisse des Depots*). The management council of the F.D.E.S. effectively controls all important investment decisions, although the proportion of investment financed through the F.D.E.S. has fallen. The *Caisse* is the plan's investment bank [99] and all its loans have to be in the framework of the plan. The Finance Minister chairs the management council of the F.D.E.S. (of which the Planning Commissioner is a member) and he retains a veto power over the activities of the *Caisse*. It has therefore been important for plan implementation that the C.G.P. and the M.E.F. work in harmony.

Cohen [101] has pointed out that during the early post-war period it was almost impossible to finance a large investment without government support since little self-finance was available and borrowing in the weak capital market was relatively costly. Thus plan implementation was possible through the control of investment funds. But although by the end of the 1950s about half of investment was financed out of borrowing, mainly from government agencies, increased self-financing lessened the dependence on the state. Government investment finance was transformed from a control to an incentive to adhere to the plan.

During the 'liberal' period of 1959-63 the main emphasis was placed on endogeneous instruments of implementation.

It was during the 1960s that considerable attention came to be paid to contractual agreements between government and industry. Such contracts have taken various forms. For example, in the early 1960s loose quasi-contracts involved the provision of finance for specific investments, but few were entered into. More important have been 'programme contracts' and 'concerted action programmes'. The former, introduced in 1966, consist of binding contracts between government and firms or trading associations granting freedom to raise prices to finance investment, provided output, investment and export plans conform to the plan's objectives. Concerted action programmes, for example that put into effect in 1966 in the steel industry, entail the provision of funds (grants) for modernisation and rationalisation of industry and consist of agreements between the government and trade association involved. Contractual agreements have also been adopted with nationalised industries in relation to wages and prices [109]. Hayward has interpreted contractual agreements in both the public and private sectors as attempts by the French government to shift part of the responsibility for economic management to industry [110].

The 1960s also saw innovations in monitoring the progress of the plans. The Fifth Plan, conceived as an outline of medium-term economic policy, set up a series of 'indicators of alert' to act as an early-warning system that the plan's targets were in danger. The indicators were intended to flash when short-run policy changes were needed if the medium-term objectives were to be achieved and to act as a psychological influence to modify the actions of private decision-makers. They were a response to the impact outside events could have on the plan in the context of exposure to international competition within the E.E.C. The indicators related to crucial thresholds in the price level, the balance of payments, G.D,P., productive investment and unemployment. In the event, it transpired that some indicators were too sensitive and others worked too slowly. The Sixth Plan introduced some new features into the monitoring system which can be summed up as a change from 'flashing lights' to 'passive' indicators [6]. The Sixth Plan system distinguishes between indicators designed to monitor key objectives (notably industrial competitiveness), those to monitor changes in the international environment and those monitoring the key conditions for realising the plan's main objectives. To avoid the over-sensitivity of some of the Fifth Plan's indicators to short-tern fluctuations not significantly endangering the plan, the indicators were calculated quarterly instead of monthly. There were no thresholds associated with the indicators so as to emphasise the absence of any automatic policy or target revision. The use of the indicators is mainly the psychological one of publicising the plan and keeping its objectives in the minds of policy-makers. Of far more importance for policy or target revisions are the annual reviews of plan implementation carried out by the Plan Commissions [94].

Hayward [99] has made the general observation that none of the French plans so far has been implemented without a major hitch, as evidenced, for example, by the introduction of the Interim Plan of 1960-1 during the Third Plan and the modification of the Fourth Plan by the Stabilisation Plan of 1963. However, assessing whether plans have been successfully implemented or not is no simple matter. Lutz [7] has criticised not only the theoretical foundations but also the practice of French planning. She has tried to demonstrate, by a comparison between predicted and realised figures for the terminal year of the plan, that French planning has not worked. This approach to assessing the success or failure of indicative planning has been severely criticised as not being the appropriate test [94, 111, 112]. The main argument that has been put forward is that Lutz's measure is a forecast-realisation index and not a plan-implementation test, since even the realisation of a forecast does not imply that a plan has been consciously perfectly implemented. A view now widely held is that only a detailed microeconomic analysis on a firm-by-firm basis can determine whether a plan has been successfully implemented. McArthur and Scott's monumental study of French industrial planning comes nearest to the latter approach. They concluded that the influence of national planning on industry was generally low, a view disputed by Massé in his introductory comments to their book [111].

The approach adopted by Vasconcellos and Kiker [108] was neither a detailed microeconomic study nor a forecast-realisation study. They examined the performance of the French economy over the period 1949-64 and tried to indicate where planning may have been influential whilst recognising the difficulty of attributing any successes to planning itself. They concluded that the French economy under planning performed very well. Growth was stable and relatively fast (averaging between 4.5 and 5.5 per cent p.a.), high rates of productivity growth were achieved with the efficient use of capital and labour and high levels of employment were maintained. However, the record for the balance of payments and price stability was less good. During the 1970s France, like other industrial countries, has suffered a slowing down in the rate of growth and an increase in unemployment as well as suffering from inflation and balance-of-payments problems. Nevertheless, the Seventh Plan is optimistic that these problems can be solved by 1980.

Although the French have now embarked on a Seventh Plan, planning having been a permanent feature in the French economy since the mid-1960s, the nature of French planning has not remained unchanged. The French approach has been pragmatic and the planners have continually responded to changing circumstances. The first two plans, in the absence of adequate statistics and well-developed planning techniques, were relatively unsophisticated. The Monnet Plan was a pragmatic response to the problems of post-war reconstruction and, together with the Second Plan, laid the foundations for fast growth. By the Third Plan statistical data, forecasting techniques and a planning theory had developed and the Fourth Plan represented a technically sophisticated and detailed plan backed up by a well-formulated theory of indicative planning. But entry into the E.E.C. had begun to be responded to by the planners [113] as the economy became more open. The early 1960s saw French planning take on a 'new look' [7], largely as a response to the new conditions the E.E.C. imposed on the French economy. The 'new look', fashioned by Massé [3] and incorporated into the Fifth Plan, distinguished clearly between plan targets (the larger aggregates) and mere forecasts (the sectoral figures for industry) and placed more emphasis on the plan's flexibility. The increased importance of prices and exports was reflected by the greater attention paid to the removal of impediments to competitiveness. The Sixth Plan, based on a new theory (of the 'competitioned' economy) and sophisticated techniques (FIFI), epitomised the move away from a demand-side expectations approach to one based on supply factors and the need for greater industrial competitiveness.

THE U.K. PLANNING EXPERIMENT

Indicative planning in France in the 1960s attracted attention in other West European countries and, to a limited extent, the E.E.C. itself [113]. The willingness of French planners to explain their system to the British has been interpreted by Leruez [114] to be part of their attempt to convert the E.E.C. to planning, in response to its impact on France itself, although at the time the United Kingdom was a potential rather than an actual E.E.C. member.

Unlike in France, early post-war planning in the United Kingdom [115] was replaced in the 1950s by a more *laissez-faire* philosophy. But by the 1960s there was dissatisfaction with both the instability of growth ('stop-go') and the slow rate of growth of the U.K. economy compared with most other Western countries. Of the latter, the French approach to growth was seen as a possible model. A London conference on French Planning, organised by the National Institute of Economic and Social Research, took place in early 1961 attended by British officials and industrialists with papers given by leading French planners (notably Massé). A summary of the papers and discussions was made widely available by Political and Economic Planning (P.E.P.) [98] and the conference contributed to the growing feeling that indicative planning might provide a solution to the United Kingdom's economic problems. That leading industrialists were in favour of planning was evident from the F.B.I. conference held at Brighton the previous year and at which proposals had been made that government and industry should discuss and agree upon an assessment of expectations for the next five years. Also, the government's advisory body, of three 'wise men', the Council on Prices, Productivity and Incomes, which had been set up in 1957, pointed the way, in its final report (1961), towards indicative planning and suggested that it should be replaced by a larger body [116]. In his crisis budget speech in the summer of 1961 the Chancellor of the Exchequer, after announcing short-term deflationary 'stop' measures in response to a balance-of-payments deficit and sterling crisis, announced that he intended to consult with both sides of industry to formulate procedures for securing planned growth [117, 118]. The outcome was the National Economic Development Council (N.E.D.C.), which was set up in February 1962 and met for the first time in March 1962.

The N.E.D.C. was set up, not as a part of the administration, but under its aegis. The membership of the N.E.D.C. reflected its role as a forum where both sides of industry could meet with the government to examine economic performance and the obstacles to growth and to come to agreement on the way to secure faster growth. The Council, as originally constituted, was chaired by the Chancellor and included two other ministers, six industrialists from the private sector and two from the nationalised industries, six trade unionists, two academic economists and the Director-General of the National Economic Development Office (N.E.D.O.). The Office's function was to carry out the programme of work laid down by the Council, which itself met monthly. The Office was set up with two main divisions, one concerned with relations with industry and the other with economic policy, including planning for growth.

In 1963 the N.E.D.C. published two reports, *The Growth of the U.K. Economy to 1966* [119] and *Conditions Favourable to Faster Growth* [120]. The first report studied the implications of an average annual growth rate of 4 per cent for the period 1961-6. The second report highlighted eight main problems and made general policy statements about each of them. The base year of 1961 for the N.E.D.C. 'plan' was chosen because it was the latest year for which reliable statistics were available [115]. The 4 per cent figure was a rough estimate arrived at by the N.E.D.O. [89]. It appears to have been chosen somewhat arbitrarily. 4 per cent represented a faster rate than that recently achieved in the United Kingdom but a rate achieved by other Western countries. Any higher growth rate would have entailed insuperable balance-of-payments problems. Academic economists at the time estimated that about 3¼ per cent would have been more realistic [121]. The report consisted of an industrial inquiry and a macroeconomic study. Both were intended to test the feasibility of the 4 per cent rate. Only seventeen industries were covered by the industrial inquiry. In selecting the industries, weight was given to their importance in the economy, the need to include both fast- and slow-growing industries, and the need to include a reasonable cross-section of industry in terms of consumer goods, capital goods and service industries in both the private and public sectors. The inquiry covered about one-half of industrial production, two-fifths of G.N.P., two-fifths of visible exports and one-half of total expenditure on fixed investment (excluding dwellings). Industry, mainly through trade associations, was asked to provide information about existing plans, the implications for the industry of a 4 per cent growth rate, and information about particular problems and how to overcome them. The inquiry asked for forecasts of output, exports, imports, employment and investment. For reasons of consistency the industries were provided with a number of common assumptions, for example that the rest of the economy would progress in a way consistent with achieving 4 per cent, that the international environment would remain the same, and that the United Kingdom would join the E.E.C. about half-way through the planning period. The results of the inquiry indicated the feasibility of the 4 per cent rate. In fact, on the basis of the information provided, the N.E.D.C. estimated that their total output would increase by 4.8 per cent p.a. so that the rest of the economy need not even have grown at 4 per cent for the average annual rate to be achieved.

The N.E.D.C. plan's industrial inquiry had a number of limitations. Bailey [117] has argued that using trade associations as a source of industry information does not always provide an accurate picture of an industry's views. He also argued that the attempt to achieve consistency was over-emphasised at the expense of reality. Indeed the report itself recognised that some of the estimates were possibly subject to substantial error.

The macroeconomic testing of the 4 per cent rate aimed to assess its feasibility in terms of manpower, productivity, consumption, investment and savings, imports, exports and the balance of payments. The labour-force estimate was of 0.8 per cent p.a. increase, and productivity was estimated to increase at 3.2 per cent p.a. (compared to 2.5 per cent p.a. for 1957-61). Public consumption and private consumption were both estimated to grow at 3.5 per cent p.a., investment by 5.3 per cent, exports by 5 per cent and imports by 4 per cent. For personal consumption per head the implication was for an annual rise of 2.9 per cent compared to 2.1 per cent in previous years, but, significantly, a rate of increase less than G.N.P. itself. However, the main issue was whether the balance of payments could stand the strain of a 4 per cent growth rate. A surplus of £300 million on the current account was envisaged by 1966 although the account was in deficit in 1961. Given an estimated 4 per cent p.a. increase in imports, to achieve the plan it was necessary for exports to grow at 5 per cent p.a. even though they had only been growing at 3 per cent. The balance-of-payments estimates were extremely optimistic and the plan side-stepped the main constraint on growth. Although the N.E.D.C. report argued that the 4 per cent rate was feasible, it has been suggested [89] that what the N.E.D.C. plan showed, but failed to recognise, was the unlikelihood of the U.K. economy, given its lack of competitiveness, being able to grow at 4 per cent p.a. between 1961 and 1966.

The second report of the N.E.D.C. was a general attempt

to examine the obstacles to growth, but the policy suggestions were not related specifically to the N.E.D.C. plan's 4 per cent growth figure. In 1964 the N.E.D.C. produced a third report, *The Growth of the Economy* [122], which was an assessment of the economy a year after the publication of the plan, by which time it was becoming clear that balance-of-payments problems were manifesting themselves.

The N.E.D.C. reports attest to the fact that it did perform the functions it was set up to carry out. How successfully it did so is difficult to assess. Following Polanyi [116] attempts have been made to use a comparison of the N.E.D.C. plan forecasts with actual outurns [114, 115]. However, such exercises are largely meaningless. To make forecast-realisation comparisons is an inappropriate plan-implementation test especially when the plan is not one to which the government is committed (the N.E.D.C. plan was not binding on the Conservative government which set the N.E.D.C. up) and when the government is replaced by a different one with its own plan. Nevertheless, this is not to argue that the N.E.D.C. plan was without defects. However, when viewed as a forum for information exchange between both sides of industry and the government, and as a pressure group for growth, the N.E.D.C. had a good measure of success.

When the Labour government, committed to planning, came to office in 1964 the Department of Economic Affairs (D.E.A.) was established as a planning ministry and the N.E.D.C. was reorganised. The D.E.A. was organised into functional divisions concerned with economic planning, economic co-ordination, industrial policies and regional policy. Most of model-builders of the economic-policy division of the N.E.D.C. moved into the D.E.A. as did many of the Treasury's forecasters, thus concentrating forecasting and planning within the D.E.A. itself. But it was recognised that there was still need for an outside body, not to prepare a national plan, but to act as a forum where both sides of industry could meet with the government and discuss policies for growth and the implications of the national plan. Thus the N.E.D.C. was retained but in a new form. The First Secretary of State for Economic Affairs (George Brown, head of the D.E.A.) replaced the Chancellor of the Exchequer as Chairman of the N.E.D.C., the Chancellor ceasing even to be a member. Thus the minister responsible for short-term economic management was excluded from the N.E.D.C. discussions of medium-term planning. Although the D.E.A. was given senior status it needed the co-operation of the Treasury to achieve its medium-term objectives, but what emerged was a rivalry between the two ministries.

The D.E.A., upon its formation, set about producing the National Plan. The Plan was prepared in essentially the same way, by essentially the same people, as the N.E.D.C. plan. The whole exercise was completed in less than a year.

The industrial inquiry was conducted through trade associations and the Economic Development Councils (E.D.C.s) for individual industries. The E.D.C.s had begun to be set up in 1964, and were charged with the job of providing forecasts and assessments of the industrys' performance and suggesting ways of improving that performance. Their composition of management, union, government and independent experts reflects the idea of a concerted approach to improving industrial performance. The questionnaire sought, on the assumption of a 25 per cent increase in national output between 1964 and 1970, estimates of output both for the home market and for exports, imports, the use of materials and fuels, manpower and investment. The coverage of the inquiry was wider than the N.E.D.C. inquiry, extending to most of the economy. The industrial inquiry came in for scathing criticism by Brunner [123], who argued that asking industry to assume a 25 per cent increase in growth was not helpful to them, and produced figures to show that consecutive equal periods with the same increase in national income reveal large changes in the income elasticity of demand for the same products. Thus any estimates of industry output based on an assumed growth of national income would be open to considerable error. The manpower, materials and investment requirements for each industry, based on the output figure, would then themselves be erroneous. It was argued that the speed with which answers to the questionnaire had to be returned did not enable reliable forecasts to be made. However, to argue against the value of forecasting in such a condemnatory manner is to ignore the fact that by the mid-1960s U.K. industry was not without experience in microeconomic forecasting.

The National Plan [124], covering the period 1964-70, was published in September 1965. In Part One of the Plan an outline of the plan, including a 'check-list' of actions necessary for plan fulfilment, was follwed by an analysis of the basis for growth in terms of output, productivity, manpower, industrial efficiency, investment, prices and incomes, the balance of payments and regional planning. An analysis of industrial sectors was followed by a section on the use of resources, which presented a picture of the planned change in terms of national output, the balance of payments, investment and consumption. Part Two of *The National Plan* contained the industry annexes, which recorded the results of the industrial inquiry.

The target for the economy was a 25 per cent increase in national output between 1964 and 1970. This was equivalent to an average 3.8 per cent annual growth rate, although the Plan envisaged an acceleration from a rate lower than this in the early years to a 4 per cent rate well before 1970. This rate of growth was dependent upon a rise in productivity of 3.4 per cent and a manpower growth of 0.4 per cent p.a. Fixed investment was to rise at 5.5 per cent with the industrial-investment component increasing at 7 per cent p.a. The planned rate of growth of exports was 5¼ per cent with imports expected to grow by only 4 per cent p.a.

The Plan revealed a manpower gap of 400,000 workers, this being the difference between the expected increase of 400,000 and the figure of 800,000 workers needed derived from the industrial inquiry. The planners optimistically believed that the gap could be reduced by mobilising 200,000 additional workers from the regions. Looked at another way, the manpower gap implied that industry did not expect productivity to increase at the rate necessary for the 25 per cent growth target to be achieved. Although the Plan envisaged a 3.4 per cent p.a. productivity rise, it emphasised that to achieve it a great effort was needed by management and workers, as well as by government efforts, to improve efficiency.

A crucial deficiency in the Plan was its inadequate analysis of the balance-of-payments problem. The objective was a surplus of £250 million. On the import side, despite the higher rate of growth of output envisaged, it was expected that over the period of the Plan the volume of imports would rise at the same rate as it had between 1960 and 1964. The target for imports was an annual increase of 4 per cent. This was based mainly on an analysis of the main commodity groups which optimistically expected a favourable change in the relationship between output growth and import growth. On the export side, the Plan moved by dubious logic from an existing rate of growth of 3 per cent p.a., *via* a forecast rate of 4 per cent, to a planned rate of 5¼ per cent. The 4 per cent forecast was based on an extrapolation of trends adjusted for an optimistically favourable change in the geographical and commodity composition of exports. The 5¼ per cent increase was required to achieve the Plan's objectives. The Plan stressed that the industrial inquiry had confirmed that such a rate of increase was possible, yet industry had been asked to compile their forecasts not only on the basis of the assumption of a 25 per cent increase in national output but on an indication that exports would have to increase twice as fast as in the past if the output growth was to be achieved [114]. Even a sympathetic analysis of the Plan concluded that the feasibility of the planned rate of growth had not been demonstrated [125].

The Plan was presented as a statement of government policy, a commitment to action by the government, and as a guide to action. The economic power of the government was referred to and it was made clear that it would be used to secure faster growth not only in the public sector but in the private sector also. However, it was stressed that most of industry and commerce would continue to be governed by market forces and that planning and the market were complementary. It was argued that by disaggregating the 25 per cent growth rate into the implications for particular industries, the Plan would help firms and industries to make better decisions. As a guide to action the 'check-list' set out what needed to be done and by whom in respect of the balance of payments, industrial efficiency, manpower policy, regional policy, public spending and periodic reviews of the Plan. What was crucially lacking, however, was a clear quantitative statement of the relationship between the policies outlined and the Plan's targets.

The National Plan was abandoned in as short a time as it had taken to prepare. In the summer of 1966, faced with balance-of-payments difficulties and a sterling crisis, severe deflationary measures were taken and the Plan was abandoned. Brittan [126] has argued that the reason the Plan failed was not just wrong figuring, nor because the internal objectives were over-optimistic, but because of the balance of payments it was impossible for the government to avoid deflating demand expectations. The Plan was devoid of any convincing balance-of-payments strategy. It has been strongly argued that the Plan's balance-of-payments objectives could only have been achieved by a planned devaluation [114, 127]. Devaluation would have facilitated the achievement of the Plan's balance-of-payments objectives, but the government chose to maintain the exchange value of the pound. In the event, after abandoning the Plan the government was forced to devalue in 1967.

The failure of the Plan revealed the dangers of transplanting an approach to growth from one economy into another. A demand-expectations approach was suitable for France during the 1950s, when growth was not constrained by supply factors and where appropriate policies were implemented to prevent the balance of payments from restricting growth [89]. Such conditions were not met in the U.K. economy in the 1960s. Moreover, by the 1960s the French had developed the institutions necessary for concerted planning to work yet the British attempted such planning without the benefit of such institutional experience. Although the N.E.D.O. may be compared with the C.G.P. and the E.D.C.s with the Plan Commissions, the former was only instituted in 1962 and the latter were few in number even at the time of preparing the National Plan. As in France the British faced the problem of reconciling short-term management of the economy with medium-term planning. The former head of the D.E.A. has indicated how financial control won the day, the government not giving priority to the Plan, thus depriving it of the possibility of success [128].

Anti-planners such as Jewkes saw planning as an ordeal [129] and a peril [6]. Polanyi [116] regarded the planning attempts as an escalation from semi-official planning, via the government's National Plan to possibly Soviet-type planning. Both Jewkes and Polanyi argued that indicative planning was bound to fail because of what they believed to be the absence of any reasonable theoretical foundations.

Whatever the reasons for the failure of planning, culminating in the abandonment of the National Plan, it was widely agreed that its failure meant the end of planning in the United Kingdom for many years to come [114, 126, 127].

Before the D.E.A. was abolished in 1969, it produced *The Task Ahead* [130], which was an economic assessment to 1972. *The Task Ahead* presented itself, not as a plan, but as a planning document to be viewed as a basis for consultations between government and both sides of industry. Three possible growth rates were put up for consultation—the 'wedge' approach, indicating a range of possible outcomes with the upper and lower lines of the wedge depicting not actual growth rates but annual average growth rates of approximately 3 per cent and 4 per cent with an increase of around 3¼ per cent presented as the most likely rate between 1968 and 1972. Barker and Lecomber [131], whilst critical of a treatment of the balance of payments similar to that in the

National Plan, regarded the over-all approach as more realistic. *The Task Ahead* was followed in 1970 by a revised assessment of prospects to 1972 [132], issued by the Treasury, which since the demise of the D.E.A. had been responsible for medium-term planning. The revision suggested possible growth rates of 3 and 3¾ per cent, reflecting the concern over the lack of progress of the economy, particularly in productive investment.

After a Conservative interlude, 1974 saw the return of a Labour government, which, towards the end of 1975 and after discussions in the N.E.D.C., produced proposals for its industrial strategy [133]. The strategy set as its aim the transforming of a declining economy into a high-output economy through improving industrial performance. The idea of a new national plan was rejected, although the earlier abandonment of planning was referred to as a reason for the existing lack of strategy. The first step in the strategy was to be a systematic statistical analysis at the microeconomic and macroeconomic levels. The statistical framework was to provide the basis for the government to make an initial assessment in order to identify the sectors most important for achieving the government's objectives. This was seen as a starting-point for developing the government's own industrial policy and as a framework for discussions between government and both sides of industry at the national, industry and firm level, through the N.E.D.C., the E.D.C.s and planning agreements. The latter were conceived as voluntary agreements between government and firms based on consent, the firm receiving various forms of assistance to act in conformity with the government's objectives. Such agreements are reminiscent of the contracts which the French have used, as is the emphasis on industrial competitiveness [100]. However, the basic difference between the current French and U.K. approaches is the absence in the United Kingdom of a national plan itself.

Bibliography

[1] L. Robbins, *The Theory of Economic Policy* (London: Macmillan, 1952).
[2] S. K. Nath, *A Perspective of Welfare Economics* (London: Macmillan, 1973).
[3] P. Masse, 'The French Plan and Economic Theory', *Econometrica* (1965).
[4] J. Black, 'The The Theory of Indicative Planning', *Oxford Economic Papers* (1968).
[5] R. Harrod, 'Are Monetary and Fiscal Policies Enough?', *Economic Journal* (1964).
[6] J. Jewkes, 'The Perils of Planning', *Three Banks Review* (1965).
[7] V. Lutz, *Central Planning for the Market Economy* (London: Longmans, 1969).
[8] G. B. Richardson, 'Planning and Competition', *Soviet Studies* (1971).
[9] J. E. Meade, *The Theory of Indicative Planning* (Manchester University Press, 1970).
[10] P. R. Gregory and R. C. Stuart, *The Soviet Economy: Structure and Performance* (New York: Harper & Row, 1974), ch. 9.
[11] J. Kornai, *Anti-Equilibrium* (Amsterdam: North-Holland, 1971).
[12] B. Csikos-Nagy, 'Macrostructural and Microstructural Performance of the Economy', *Soviet Studies* (1971-2).
[13] N. Spulber, 'On Some Issues in the Theory of the "Socialist Economy",' *Kyklos* (1972).
[14] W. Keizer, *The Soviet Quest for Economic Rationality* (Rotterdam University Press, 1971).
[15] L. Hurwicz, 'Centralization and Decentralization in Economic Systems', *American Economic Review* (1969).
[16] J. Kornai and T. Liptak, 'Two-level Planning', *Econometrica* (1965).

[17] P. S. Albin, 'Uncertainty, Information Exchange and the Theory of Indicative Planning', *Economic Journal* (1971).
[18] R. Lecomber, 'Government Planning, With and Without the Cooperation of Industry', *Economics of Planning* (1970).
[19] J. Montias and T. Koopmans, 'On the Description and Comparison of Economic Systems', in *Comparison of Economic Systems,* ed. A. Eckstein (University of California Press, 1971).
[20] R. D. Portes, 'The Strategy and Tactics of Economic Decentralisation', *Soviet Studies* (1971).
[21] M. Bornstein (ed.), *Plan and Market: Economic Reform in Eastern Europe* (Yale University Press, 1973).
[22] J. G. Zielinski, 'Economics and Politics of Economic Reforms in Eastern Europe', *Economics of Planning* (1969).
[23] R. D. Portes, 'Decentralised Planning Procedures and Centrally Planned Economies', *American Economic Review* (1971).
[24] M. Lavigne, *The Socialist Economies of the Soviet Union and Europe* (London: Martin Robertson, 1974).
[25] M. Bornstein, 'Soviet Price Theory and Policy', in *The Soviet Economy,* ed. M. Bornstein and D. R. Fusfeld, (New York: Irwin-Dorsey, 1974).
[26] A. Zauberman, *Aspects of Planometrics* (University of London: Athlone Press, 1967).
[27] R. W. Campbell, *Soviet Type Economies* (London: Macmillan, 1974).
[28] M. Bornstein and D. R. Fusfeld (eds), *The Soviet Economy* (New York: Irwin-Dorsey, 1974) ch. 15A,B.
[29] J. Wilczynski, *The Economics of Socialism* (London: Macmillan, 1972).
[30] C. W. Lawson, 'The Soviet Approach to Development', *Economics* (1972).
[31] E. Domar, 'A Soviet Model of Growth', in *Socialist Economics,* ed. A. Nove and D. Nuti (Harmondsworth: Penguin, 1972).

[32] A. Erlich, *The Soviet Industrialization Debate, 1924-8* (Harvard University Press, 1960).
[33] A. Nove, *An Economic History of the USSR* (London: Allen Lane, 1969).
[34] A. Erlich, 'Development Strategy and Planning: The Soviet Experience', in *National Economic Planning*, ed. M. F. Millikan (New York: National Bureau of Economic Research, 1967).
[35] J. A. Yunker, 'A Survey of Market Socialist Forms', *Annals of Public and Cooperative Economy* (1975).
[36] J. Drewnowski, 'The Economic Theory of Socialism: A Suggestion for Consideration', *Journal of Political Economy* (1961).
[37] G. Feiwel, 'On the Economic Theory of Socialism: Some Reflections on Lange's Contributions', *Kyklos* (1972).
[38] W. Brus, *The Market in a Socialist Economy* (London: Routledge & Kegan Paul, 1972).
[39] M. Dobb, 'On Economic Theory and Socialism', in *Socialist Economics*, ed. A. Nove and D. Nuti (Harmondsworth: Penguin, 1972).
[40] O. Sik, *Plan and Market Under Socialism* (New York: International Arts and Sciences Press, 1967).
[41] B. Ward, *The Socialist Economy* (New York: Random House, 1967).
[42] J. Vanek, *The General Theory of Labor-Managed Market Economics* (Cornell University Press, 1970).
[43] J. R. Shackleton, 'IS Workers' Self-Management the Answer?, *National Westminster Bank Review* (1976).
[44] B. Csikos-Nagy, *Socialist Economic Policy* (London: Longmans, 1973).
[45] M. Kalecki, 'Outline of a Method of Constructing a Perspective Plan', in *Socialist Economics*, ed. A. Nove and D. Nuti, (Harmondsworth: Penguin, 1972).
[46] A. Chilosi, 'The Theory of Growth of a Socialist Economy of M. Kalecki', *Economics of Planning* (1971).
[47] G. R. Feiwel, 'Towards a Theory of Growth of a Centrally Planned Economy', *Soviet Studies* (1970-1).

[48] T. Wilczynski, *Technology in Comecon* (New York: Praeger, 1974).
[49] A. Zauberman, *The Mathematical Revolution in Soviet Economics* (Oxford University Press, 1975).
[50] P. Wiles, *Political Economy of Communism* (Oxford: Blackwell, 1963).
[51] M. Ellman, *Planning Problems in the USSR* (Cambridge University Press, 1973).
[52] A. Nove and D. Nuti (eds), *Socialist Economics* (Harmondsworth: Penguin, 1972).
[53] J. P. Hardt *et al.*, *Mathematics and Computers in Soviet Economic Planning* (Yale University Press, 1967).
[54] N. Spulber, *Socialist Management and Planning* (Indiana University Press, 1971).
[55] M. J. Swann, 'On the Theory of Optimal Planning in the Soviet Union', *Australian Economic Papers* (1975).
[56] J. Kornai, 'A General Descriptive Model of Planning Processes', *Economics of Planning* (1970).
[57] J. Wilczynski, *Socialist Economic Development and Reforms* (London: Macmillan 1972).
[58] A. Nove, *The Soviet Economy* (London: Allen & Unwin, 1968).
[59] H. J. Sherman, *The Soviet Economy* (Boston: Little, Brown & Co., 1969).
[60] J. Marczewski, *Crisis in Socialist Planning* (New York: Praeger, 1974).
[61] R. W. Davies, 'Economic Planning in the USSR', in *The Soviet Economy*, ed. M. Bornstein and D. R. Fusfeld (New York: Irwin-Dorsey, 1974).
[62] J. G. Zielinski, *On the Theory of Socialist Planning* (Oxford University Press, 1968).
[63] H. Levine, 'Pressure and Planning in the Soviet Economy', in *Industrialization in Two Systems: Essays in Honor of Alexander Gerschenkron*, ed. A. Rosovsky (New York: Wiley, 1966).
[64] J. Montias, 'Planning with Material Balances', *American Economic Review* (1959).

[65] M. Ellman, 'The Consistency of Soviet Plans', *Scottish Journal of Political Economy* (1969).
[66] J. Montias, 'On the Consistency and Efficiency of Central Plans', *Review of Economic Studies* (1962).
[67] M. Ellman, *Soviet Planning Today* (Cambridge University Press, 1971).
[68] H. Levine, 'Input-Output Analysis and Soviet Planning', *American Economic Review* (1962).
[69] M. Peston, *Elementary Matrices for Economics*, (London: Routledge & Kegan Paul, 1969) ch. 3.
[70] C. Yan, *Introduction to Input-Output Economics* (New York: Holt, Rinehart & Winston, 1968).
[71] P. Weitzman, 'Soviet Long Term Consumption Planning: Distribution According to Rational Needs', *Soviet Studies* (1974).
[72] B. Miezkowski, 'Recent Discussions On Consumption Planning in Poland', *Soviet Studies* (1970-1).
[73] G. Schroeder, 'The Reform of the Supply System in Soviet Industry', *Soviet Studies* (1972).
[74] J. Wilczynski, 'Risk, Uncertainty and Modern Socialist Economies', *East African Economic Review*, (1973).
[75] H. Hunter, 'Optimum Tautness in Developmental Planning', *Economic Development and Cultural Change* (1961).
[76] M. Keren, 'On the Tautness of Plans', *Review of Economic Studies* (1972).
[77] A. Abouchar, 'Inefficiency and Reform in the Soviet Economy', *Soviet Studies* (1973).
[78] R. Clarke, 'Dr. Abouchar and Levels of Inefficiency', *Soviet Studies* (1973).
[79] T. Brada, 'Allocative Efficiency and the System of Economic Management in Some Socialist Countries', *Kyklos* (1974).
[80] M. Kaser and J. G. Zielinski, *Planning in East Europe* (London: Bodley Head, 1970).
[81] G. Schroeder, 'Soviet Economic Reforms: A Study in Contradictions', *Soviet Studies* (1968).
[82] G. Schroeder, 'Soviet Economic Reform at an Impasse', *Problems of Communism* (1971).

[83] J. G. Zielinski, 'On the Theory of Economic Reforms and their Optimal Sequence', *Economics of Planning* (1968).
[84] J. G. Zielinski, 'Economic Reforms in Eastern Europe', *Economics of Planning* (1969).
[85] H. Hohmann, M. Kaser and K. C. Thalheim (eds), *The New Economic Systems of Eastern Europe* (London: Hurst & Co., 1975).
[86] P. Massé, 'French Methods of Planning', *Journal of Industrial Economics* (1962).
[87] G. B. Richardson, *Information and Investment* (Oxford University Press, 1960).
[88] M. J. Surrey, 'The National Plan in Retrospect', *Bulletin of the Oxford University Institute of Economics and Statistics* (1972).
[89] G. Denton *et al.*, *Economic Planning and Policies in Britain, France and Germany* (London: Allen & Unwin, 1968).
[90] J. Meade, *The Controlled Economy* (London: Allen & Unwin, 1971).
[91] W. Beckerman and Associates, *The British Economy in 1975* (Cambridge University Press, 1965).
[92] S. Brittan, 'Inquest on Planning in Britain', *Planning* (1967).
[93] W. Eltis, 'Economic Growth and the British Balance of Payments', *District Bank Review* (1967).
[94] D. Liggins, *National Economic Planning in France* (Farnborough: Saxon House, 1975).
[95] R. Courbis, 'The Fifi Model Used in the Preparation of the French Plan', *Economics of Planning* (1972).
[96] A. Shonfield, *Modern Capitalism* (Oxford University Press, 1965).
[97] J. and A. Hackett, *Economic Planning In France*, (London: Allen & Unwin, 1963).
[98] P. Massé, 'The Guiding Ideas behind French Planning', in 'Economic Planning in France', *Planning* (1961).
[99] J. Hayward, *The One and Indivisible French Republic* (London: Weidenfeld & Nicolson, 1973).

[100] D. Liggins, 'What Can We Learn from French Planning?', *Lloyds Bank Review* (1976).
[101] S. Cohen, *Modern Capitalist Planning* (London: Weidenfeld & Nicolson, 1969).
[102] J. Hayward, 'The Politics of Planning in France and Britain', *Comparative Politics* (1975).
[103] J. Hayward, *Private Interests and Public Policy* (London: Longmans, 1966).
[104] M. MacLennan, 'French Planning: Some Lessons for Britain', *Planning* (1963).
[105] J. Drèze, 'Some Postwar Contributions of French Economists to Theory and Public Policy', *American Economic Review*, supplement (1964).
[106] United Nations, *Multi-level Planning and Decision-making* (New York, 1970).
[107] C. Kindleberger in *National Economic Planning*, ed. M. Millikan (Columbia University Press, 1967) ch. 8.
[108] A. Vasconcellos and B. Kiker, 'An Evaluation of French National Planning: 1949-64', *Journal of Common Market Studies* (1969-70).
[109] O.E.C.D., *The Industrial Policy of France* (Paris, 1974).
[110] J. Hayward, 'State Intervention in France: The Changing Style of Government and Industry Relations', *Political Studies* (1972).
[111] J. McArthur and B. Scott, *Industrial Planning in France* (Harvard University Press, 1969).
[112] J. Hough, 'French Economic Policy', *National Westminster Bank Review* (1976).
[113] G. Denton, *Planning in the EEC: The Medium-term Economic Policy Programme of the European Economic Community*, Political and Economic Planning (London: Chatham House, 1967).
[114] J. Leruez, *Economic Planning and Politics in Britain* (London: Martin Robertson, 1975).
[115] C. Sandford, *National Economic Planning* (London: Heinemann, 1972).
[116] G. Polanyi, *Planning in Britain* (London: Institute of Economic Affairs, 1967).

[117] R. Bailey, *Managing the British Economy* (London: Hutchinson, 1968).
[118] J. Mitchell, *Groundwork to Economic Planning* (London: Weidenfeld & Nicolson, 1966).
[119] N.E.D.C., *The Growth of the U.K. Economy to 1966* (London: H.M.S.O., 1963).
[120] N.E.D.C., *Conditions Favourable to Faster Growth* (London: H.M.S.O., 1963).
[121] A. Day, 'The Myth of Four Per Cent Growth', *Westminster Bank Review (1964).*
[122] *N.E.D.C., The Growth of the Economy* (London: H.M.S.O., 1964).
[123] J. Brunner, *The National Plan* (London: Institute of Economic Affairs, 1965).
[124] D.E.A.,*The National Plan* (London: H.M.S.O., 1965).
[125] G. Denton, 'The National Plan: Its Contribution to Growth', *Planning* (1965).
[126] S. Brittan, 'Inquest on Planning in Britain', *Planning* (1967).
[127] W. Beckerman (ed.), *The Labour Governments' Economic Record: 1964-70* (London: Duckworth, 1972).
[128] G. Brown, *In My Way* (London: Gollanz, 1971).
[129] J. Jewkes, *The New Ordeal by Planning* (London: Macmillan, 1968).
[130] D.E.A., *The Task Ahead: Economic Assessment to 1972* (London: H.M.S.O. 1969).
[131] T. Barker and R. Lecomber, 'Economic Planning for 1972: An Appraisal of the Task Ahead', *Planning* (1969).
[132] H. M. Treasury, *Economic Prospects to 1972: A Revised Assessment* (London: H.M.S.O., 1970).
[133] Treasury/Department of Industry, *An Approach to Industrial Strategy* (London: H.M.S.O., 1975).